STANDARD LOAN

UNLESS RECALLED BY ANOTHER READER
THIS ITEM MAY BE BORROWED FOR

FOUR WEEKS

19. JAN

Daily Book

Year 5

UNIVERSITY COLLEGE CHICHESTER

AUTHOR:

TITLE:
LITERACY

DATE: 1-01

WS 2165814 5

CR
428 EPD

SUBJECT:
CR

Every effort has been made to trace copyright holders and to
obtain their permission for the use of copyright material.
The authors and publishers would gladly receive information
enabling them to rectify any error or omission in subsequent editions.

Acknowledgements
The extract from *Peter Pan* by J.M. Barrie in a new version by John Caird and
Trevor Nunn; the extract from *The Hobbit* by J.R.R. Tolkien published by
HarperCollins Publishers Ltd; the extract from *Jim Hedgehog and the Lonesome
Tower* by Russell Hoban, published by Hamish Hamilton 1990 and David
Higham Associates as representatives of the author; the extract from *The Owl
Service* by Alan Garner published by HarperCollins Publishers Ltd; Pat Cunneen
and the Enfield Independent for the extract from *'Enfield use their Heads for
Victory'*; the extract from *The Borrowers* by Mary Norton published by Harcourt,
Brace and Company; the extract from *Philips 14 TVCR2 TV/VIDEO Combination
Instruction Booklet* by kind permission of Philips Electronics; the extract from
Egyptian Mythology by Geraldine Harris, published by the British Museum Press
(the Trustees of the British Museum, British Museum Press); *'The Diver'* by Ian
Serraillier, by kind permission of Anne Serraillier; the extract from *Looking at
Materials* by Peter Stokes, published by Nelson; the extract from *'Mr Fox'* from
A Dictionary of British Folk Tales by Katherine M. Briggs, published by
Routledge; the extract from *Exploring the World of the Pharoahs* by Christine
Hobson © 1987 published by Thames and Hudson Ltd; the extract from their
'Wildlife Facts' leaflet by kind permission of London Wildlife Trust; the extract
from *'Secrets'* by Anita Desai, published in *Guardian Angels* ed. Stephanie
Nettell, c/o Rogers, Coleridge & White Ltd; the extract from *Little House in the
Big Woods* by Laura Ingalls Wilder, copyright 1932 Laura Ingalls Wilder,
renewed 1959 by Roger L. Macbride, reprinted by permission of Harper & Row
Publishers Inc. and by permission of Methuen Children's Books, Reed Consumer
Books Ltd; the extract from their brochure by kind permission of Redwings
Horse Sanctuary; the extract from *'Night Mail'* by W. H. Auden, published by
Faber & Faber; *'Hunter Poems of the Yoruba'* from *The Rattle Bag* eds. Seamus
Heaney and Ted Hughes, published by Faber & Faber; the extract from *Carrie's
War* by Nina Bowden published by Penguin Books Ltd; *'Reynard the Fox'* by John
Masefield by kind permission of the Society of Authors as the Literary
Representative of the author; the extract from their leaflet reprinted by kind
permission of the PDSA. *'Slowly the fog'* and *'Mist'* from *English through
Experience* eds. A.W. Rowe and Peter Emmens.

The painting on page 72, MAM68945 00294 *Children's Games* (Kinderspiele),
1560 (panel) by Peiter the Elder Brueghel (c. 1515-69), is reprinted by
permission of the Kunsthistorisches Museum, Vienna/Bridgeman Art Library,
London/New York

First published 1998
Reprinted 1998 (three times), 1999 (twice), 2000

Letts Educational, Schools and Colleges Division,
9-15 Aldine Street, London W12 8AW
Tel: 020 8740 2266   Fax: 020 8743 8451

Text © Ray Barker and Louis Fidge
Designed, edited and produced by Gecko Limited, Bicester, Oxon
Illustrations © Richard Adams (The Inkshed), Kiran Ahmad,
Sally Artz, James Bartholomew, Jonathan Bentley (Beint &
Beint), David Frankland (Artist Partners), Gecko Limited,
Doreen McGuiness, Dave Mostyn, Robert McPhillips,
Dave Pattison, Martin Sanders, Ron Tiner, Clara Urquijo.

All our rights reserved. No part of this publication may
be reproduced, stored in a retrieval system, or transmitted, in any form or by
any means, electronic, mechanical, photocopying, recording or otherwise,
without prior permission of Letts Educational.

British Library Cataloguing-in-Publication Data
A CIP record for this book is available from the British Library

ISBN 184085 0655
Printed in Spain by Mateu Cromo

Letts Educational Ltd, a division of Granada Learning Ltd. Part of the Garanda
Media Group.
Visit www.letts-education.com for free education and revision advice.

Introduction

The Literacy Textbooks:

- support the teaching of the Literacy Hour
- help meet the majority of the objectives of the National Literacy Strategy Framework
- are divided into 3 sections, each sufficient for one term's work
- contain ten units per term, each equivalent to a week's work
- provide two Self Assessment units in each term to check on progress
- contain two Writing Focus units each term to support compositional writing
- include a Glossary of definitions of terms used in the book
- list High Frequency Words at the back of the Year 3, 4 and 5 textbooks
- provide coverage of a wide range of writing, both fiction and non-fiction as identified in the National Literacy Strategy Framework.

Unit number →

Text for reading and discussion

Key teaching points

Text Level activities (purple)

Sentence Level activities (yellow)

Word Level activities (green)

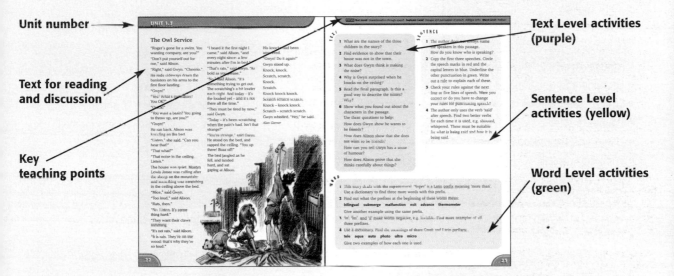

Self Assessment units:

- appear after every five units
- review the key objectives at Sentence Level and Word Level in the preceding five units
- contain a spelling chart to support the teaching of spelling strategies
- may be used to provide:
  - a review of progress when completed and kept as a record
  - further practice in areas of concern
  - homework assignments.

The Glossary:

- explains and gives examples of key words and concepts
- may be used for teaching purposes or for reference by the pupil.

Writing Focus units:

- appear after every five units of work
- develop work covered in the preceding five teaching units
- support work on compositional writing
- contain support for the teaching of different essential writing skills, e.g. how to plan a story.

High Frequency Word lists:

- contain words that occur frequently in children's reading and writing
- help children to recognise these words and to spell them correctly
- are often referred to and used in the activities in the book
- provide an easily accessible resource for spelling activities.

Text Level	Sentence Level	Word Level
• Story structure; Characterisation	Adverbs	Synonyms
• Conventions of playscripts	Dialogue	Independent spelling strategies
• Nonsense verse	Person and tenses of verbs	Idioms; Prefixes
• Characterisation; Story beginnings	Verbs and adverbs	Spelling strategies – suffixes
• Features of instructional texts	Imperatives and tenses of verbs	Plurals

Term 1

Writing Focus 1.1   Story structure; Playscripts: Giving instructions; Planning Checklist
Self Assessment 1.1   Review of Word and Sentence Level Units 1.1 – 1.5; Handy hints for spelling

Text Level	Sentence Level	Word Level
• Story openings and characterisation	Making complex sentences	Qualifying verbs
• Characterisation through speech	Dialogue, verbs, punctuation of speech	Prefixes
• Features of news reports	Verbs	Synonyms; Cliché
• Point of view	Verb tenses; Direct/reported speech	Suffixes
• Features of instructional texts	Verb tenses	Roots of words and word building

Writing Focus 1.2   News reports; Describing characters; Point of view; Writing Steps
Self Assessment 1.2   Review of Word and Sentence Level Units 1.6 – 1.10; Handy hints for spelling

Text Level	Sentence Level	Word Level
• Legends and traditional stories	Writing for different audiences	Spelling pronouns
• Stories from ancient cultures	Using commas	Spelling patterns – 'll' and 'l'
• Poems that tell a story	Agreement – noun and verb	Spelling patterns – adding 'ing'/'ed'
• Literal and figurative language	Agreement – tense and subject	Onomatopoeia
• Writing to explain	Categories of nouns	Homophones

Term 2

Writing Focus 2.1   Using poetry; Writing legends and myths; Making notes; Reviewing writing
Self Assessment 2.1   Review of Word and Sentence Level Units 2.1 – 2.5; Handy hints for spelling

Text Level	Sentence Level	Word Level
• Versions of similar stories	Nouns and pronouns	Soft and hard 'c' and 'g'
• Folk tales and myths	Summarising sentences	Antonyms
• Poetic language	Constructing sentences	Doubling the final consonant
• Writing to explain	Ambiguity	Homographs
• Locating and writing information	Agreement with verbs	Range and variety of antonyms

Writing Focus 2.2   Using poems; Myths and fairy tales; Communicating information; Editing checklist
Self Assessment 2.2   Review of Word and Sentence Level Units 2.6 – 2.10; Handy hints for spelling

Text Level	Sentence Level	Word Level
• Different cultures	Punctuation, commas	Unstressed vowels in polysyllabic words
• Story settings	Apostrophes for contraction	Spelling patterns – omit 'e'
• Writing to inform and persuade	Agreement between parts of sentences	Spelling patterns – 'i' before 'e'
• Poetry – telling a story	Phrases	Spelling patterns – 'y' to 'ies'
• Letters to persuade and argue	Clauses	Transforming words – changing tenses

Term 3

Writing Focus 3.1   Poems as models – adding dialogue; Writing an argument; Proof-reading
Self Assessment 3.1   Review of Word and Sentence Level Units 3.1 – 3.5; Handy hints for spelling

Text Level	Sentence Level	Word Level
• Ways of life – point of view	Prepositions	Words from other cultures
• Characters and their treatment	Use of commas	Transforming words – negatives
• Poetry – emotions	Apostrophes for possession	Transforming words – comparatives
• Advertising and persuasion	Connecting words used in an argument	Transforming words – parts of speech
• Poetry – point of view	Combining sentences using connectives	Dictionary work – alphabetical order

Writing Focus 3.2   Book reviews; Point of view; Describing characters; Planning a book review
Self Assessment 3.2   Review of Word and Sentence Level Units 3.6 – 3.10; Handy hints for spelling

CONTENTS

A Christmas Carol

The door of Scrooge's counting-house was open that he might keep his eye upon his clerk who, in a dismal little cell beyond, a sort of tank, was copying letters. Scrooge had a very small fire, but the clerk's fire was so very much smaller that it looked like one coal. But he couldn't replenish it, for Scrooge kept the coal-box in his own room; and so surely as the clerk came in with the shovel, the master predicted that it would be necessary for them to part. Therefore the clerk put on his white comforter, and tried to warm himself at the candle; in which effort, not being a man of strong imagination, he failed.

"A Merry Christmas, Uncle! God save you!" cried a cheerful voice. It was the voice of Scrooge's nephew, who came upon him so quickly that this was the first intimation he had of his approach.

"Bah!" said Scrooge. "Humbug!"

He had so heated himself with rapid walking in the fog and frost, this nephew of Scrooge's, that he was all in a glow; his face was ruddy and handsome; his eyes sparkled, and his breath smoked again.

"Christmas a humbug, Uncle?" said Scrooge's nephew. "You don't mean that, I'm sure?"

"I do," said Scrooge. "Merry Christmas! What right have you to be merry? What reason have you to be merry? You're poor enough."

"Come, then," returned the nephew gaily. "What right have you to be dismal? What reason have you to be morose? You're rich enough."

Scrooge, having no better answer ready on the spur of the moment, said "Bah" again; and followed it up with "Humbug".

"Don't be cross, Uncle!" said the nephew.

"What else can I be," returned the uncle, "when I live in such a world of fools as this? Merry Christmas! Out upon merry Christmas! What's Christmas time to you but a time for paying bills without money; a time for finding yourself a year older, and not an hour richer; a time for balancing your books and having every item in 'em through a round dozen of months presented dead against you? If I could work my will," said Scrooge indignantly, "every idiot who goes about with 'Merry Christmas' on his lips, should be boiled with his own pudding, and buried with a stake of holly through his heart. He should!"

Charles Dickens

TEXT

1 Where does the scene in the story take place?

2 Find three words in the passage which tell you that this book was written a long time ago. Use a dictionary. What do they mean?

3 How can you tell that Scrooge's nephew had been walking fast? Give reasons.

4 We can learn about the character of Scrooge from the story. Read the passage again. Copy and complete a chart like this.

What is in the text	What this might mean about Scrooge
door open to keep eye on clerk	suspicious, does not trust him

5 Now write a paragraph about Scrooge. Give your evidence after each point, e.g. I think Scrooge is a suspicious man because …

SENTENCE

1 Here are five verbs from the first paragraph:
'was copying', 'looked', 'came in', 'predicted', 'failed'.

Write adverbs to give us more information about the verbs, e.g. the adverb 'neatly' would tell us more about the verb 'was copying'.

2 Use a dictionary. Find five examples of adverbs that use 'more' or 'most', e.g. quickly, more quickly, most quickly.

3 Use a dictionary. Copy and complete the chart to show a different pattern:

hard	harder	hardest
badly		
much		
soon		
well		

WORD

1 Use a thesaurus. Find alternative words for 'dismal', 'cell' and 'tank', which Dickens uses in the first paragraph, e.g. 'little room' could mean the same as 'cell'. Put the words into the sentences from the passage. Say if you think your new word is better, and why.

2 Use a thesaurus to find synonyms for these words in the passage:
warm cheerful quickly walking smoked morose

3 Write a sentence to show the meaning of each synonym.

Peter Pan

(He sits on the floor with the shadow, confident that he and it will join like drops of water. Then he tries to stick it on with soap from the bathroom, and this failing also, he subsides dejectedly on the floor. This wakens Wendy, who sits up, and is pleasantly interested to see a stranger.)

Wendy: *(Courteously.)* Boy, why are you crying? *(He jumps up, and crossing to the foot of the bed bows to her in the fairy way. Wendy, impressed, bows to him from the bed.)*

Peter: What is your name?

Wendy: *(Well satisfied.)* Wendy Moira Angela Darling. What is yours?

Peter: *(Finding it lamentably brief.)* Peter Pan.

Wendy: Is that all?

Peter: *(Biting his lip.)* Yes.

Wendy: *(Politely.)* I am so sorry.

Peter: It doesn't matter.

Wendy: Where do you live?

Peter: Second on the right and then straight on till morning.

Wendy: What a funny address!

Peter: No, it isn't.

Wendy: I mean, is that what they put on the letters?

Peter: Don't get any letters.

Wendy: But your mother gets letters?

Peter: Don't have a mother.

Wendy: Peter! *(She leaps out of bed to put her arms round him, but he draws back.)*

No wonder you were crying.

Peter: I wasn't crying about my mother. I was crying because I can't get my shadow to stick on. Anyway I wasn't crying.

Wendy: It has come off! How awful. *(Looking at the spot where he had lain.)* Peter, you have been trying to stick it on with soap!

Peter: *(Snappily.)* Well, then?

Wendy: It must be sewn on.

Peter: What is 'sewn'?

Wendy: You are dreadfully ignorant.

Peter: No, I'm not.

Wendy: I will sew it on for you, my little man. Stand still. I dare say it will hurt a little.

Peter: *(A recent remark of hers rankling.)* I never cry. *(She seems to sew the shadow to his heels. He bears the pain, and then tests the combination, but the flimsy thing drags uselessly behind him.)* It isn't quite itself yet.

Wendy: Perhaps I should have ironed it.

Peter: Perhaps it's dead.

Wendy: I think we need a little more light. *(She touches something and to his astonishment the room is illuminated. The shadow awakes and is glad to be back with him as he is to have it. He and his shadow dance together.)*

J.M. Barrie, adapted by John Caird and Trevor Nunn

TEXT

1 What has Peter Pan lost?
   How is he trying to put it back?

2 Why does he wake Wendy up?
   How does she solve his problem?

3 Why is Peter's address a strange one?

4 Find two reasons to explain why
   Wendy feels sorry for Peter.

5 Find three ways a play script is
   different from speech written in a
   story, e.g.

Play	Story
No speech marks	

6 *a)* How do the actors know how to
       show what their characters are
       feeling?

   b) Write three sets of stage
       directions from *Peter Pan*. Say
       why they are written in italics and
       inside brackets.

SENTENCE

1 Write out the first four speeches of
   the script as direct speech in a story.
   What differences are there?

2 Write the next four speeches as
   direct speech, and use a different
   verb for 'said' each time, e.g. replied.
   Use a thesaurus to find more
   synonyms for 'said'.

3 Find an example of each of these
   types of dialogue from the passage.
   Copy and complete this chart.

statements	
questions	Why are you crying?
exclamations	
replies	
greetings	

WORD

1 Write five words from the passage containing one syllable only.
   Find an entire sentence containing single-syllable words.

2 How many syllables do these words contain?
   crying   morning   funny   letters   shadows   anyway   dreadfully

3 Write out the words from question 2, broken into their syllables, e.g. cry-ing.

4 Now find any smaller words in the words, e.g. 'crying' contains 'cry'.

5 Write out three words with more than one syllable. Draw boxes around the syllables.

6 Find other words containing simple suffixes such as 'ing'.
   Circle the suffixes and underline the roots of the words, e.g. crying.

The Owl and the Pussy-Cat

This poem was written over a hundred years ago.
It is called a 'nonsense poem' because some of it
seems to be very silly. When you have worked on it,
you should try reading it aloud to really enjoy it.

The Owl and the Pussy-Cat went to sea
In a beautiful pea-green boat,
They took some honey, and plenty of money,
Wrapped up in a five-pound note.
The Owl looked up to the stars above,
And sang to a small guitar,
"O lovely Pussy! O Pussy, my love,
What a beautiful pussy you are,
You are,
You are!
What a beautiful Pussy you are!"

Pussy said to the Owl, "You elegant fowl!
How charmingly sweet you sing!

O let us be married! Too long we have
tarried,
But what shall we do for a ring?"
They sailed away for a year and a day,
To the land where the Bong-tree grows,
And there in a wood a Piggy-wig stood,
With a ring at the end of his nose,
His nose,

His nose,
With a ring at the
end of his nose.

"Dear Pig, are you willing to sell for a shilling
Your ring?" Said the Piggy, "I will."
So they took it away, and were married next day
By the Turkey who lives on the hill.
They dined on mince, and slices of quince,
Which they ate with a runcible spoon;
And hand in hand, on the edge of the sand,
They danced by the light of the moon,
The moon,
The moon,
They danced by the light of the moon.

Edward Lear

TEXT

1 *a)* What colour was the Owl and the Pussy-Cat's boat?

b) What did they take with them on the trip?

2 *a)* Where did they find their wedding ring?

b) Describe how they bought it.

3 Find three words that show the poem was written over a hundred years ago. Use a dictionary and write down their meanings today.

4 *a)* Read verse 2. Which words rhyme at the ends of the lines and in the same lines?

b) What is there at the end of every verse which tells you that the poem was written to be read aloud?

5 This kind of poem is called 'nonsense verse'. List five things that you think are 'nonsense' in the poem and say if and why you find them amusing.

SENTENCE

1 Find evidence in the poem for these statements:

a) When someone is telling a story, they use the past tense.

b) When they talk about more than one person, they use the third person of the verb – 'they'.

2 Find an example in the poem of the first person of a verb being used.

3 *a)* Write out the last 4 lines of the first verse (the chorus). Use 'we' instead of 'you'. *b)* Does this make sense in the poem? Explain why not.

4 Try replacing 'we' in verse 2 with 'you'. Explain how this makes a difference to the sense of the poem.

5 Write out the final verse.

a) Underline all the verbs.

b) Change them all to the present tense.

c) Explain how this changes the meaning of the poem.

d) Which tense do you prefer? Say why.

WORD

1 Draw cartoon pictures with captions to show what these idioms actually *say*:

• **raining cats and dogs** • **turning over a new leaf** • **pull a long face** • **break your word**

2 Explain in your own words what each of the phrases really means.

3 Write what you would mean if you used these proverbs:

a) When the cat's away the mice will play. *b)* Never judge a book by the cover.

4 Add 'dis' and 'un' (negative prefixes) to these words:

appear   approve   appoint   fair   appealing

Does the spelling change?

5 Use a dictionary. Find the meanings of these Greek and Latin prefixes:

auto   bi   trans   tele   circu

Give two examples of how each one is used, e.g. <u>bi</u>cycle.

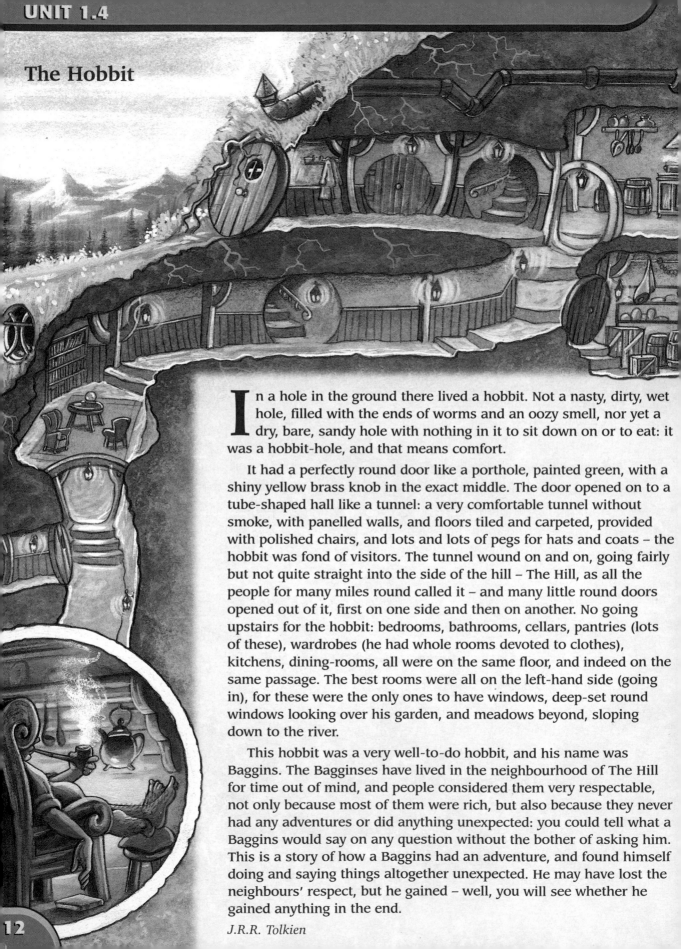

The Hobbit

I n a hole in the ground there lived a hobbit. Not a nasty, dirty, wet hole, filled with the ends of worms and an oozy smell, nor yet a dry, bare, sandy hole with nothing in it to sit down on or to eat: it was a hobbit-hole, and that means comfort.

It had a perfectly round door like a porthole, painted green, with a shiny yellow brass knob in the exact middle. The door opened on to a tube-shaped hall like a tunnel: a very comfortable tunnel without smoke, with panelled walls, and floors tiled and carpeted, provided with polished chairs, and lots and lots of pegs for hats and coats – the hobbit was fond of visitors. The tunnel wound on and on, going fairly but not quite straight into the side of the hill – The Hill, as all the people for many miles round called it – and many little round doors opened out of it, first on one side and then on another. No going upstairs for the hobbit: bedrooms, bathrooms, cellars, pantries (lots of these), wardrobes (he had whole rooms devoted to clothes), kitchens, dining-rooms, all were on the same floor, and indeed on the same passage. The best rooms were all on the left-hand side (going in), for these were the only ones to have windows, deep-set round windows looking over his garden, and meadows beyond, sloping down to the river.

This hobbit was a very well-to-do hobbit, and his name was Baggins. The Bagginses have lived in the neighbourhood of The Hill for time out of mind, and people considered them very respectable, not only because most of them were rich, but also because they never had any adventures or did anything unexpected: you could tell what a Baggins would say on any question without the bother of asking him. This is a story of how a Baggins had an adventure, and found himself doing and saying things altogether unexpected. He may have lost the neighbours' respect, but he gained – well, you will see whether he gained anything in the end.

J.R.R. Tolkien

TEXT

1 Look at the first paragraph. Write down three questions you would like to ask the author after reading it.

2 *a)* Do you think this is a good way to start a story? Why? *b)* Why do you think the author did not start his story with the last two sentences? Give reasons.

3 Who is the author talking to in these last two sentences?
Write down the word that tells you.

4 What sort of hobbit lives in this hole? Copy the chart, then read the passage and add more evidence and deductions.

Evidence	Deduction
not wet or dirty	likes comfort
shiny door knob	tidy and clean

5 Now write a paragraph which starts: 'From the evidence I believe that the hobbit who lives in this hole is … because …' and give a reason for each of your points.

SENTENCE

1 Copy these sentences. Underline the adverbs.

a) Bilbo lived quietly in his hole. *b)* He said loudly that he did not like adventures. *c)* One day he was taken suddenly into another world.

2 Imagine Bilbo Baggins is writing in his diary. What adverbs might he use? Copy and complete these sentences. Use a new adverb each time, e.g. Today I walked *quickly* to the shops.

a) Today I ate … *b)* Today I dressed … *c)* Today I laughed …

3 Now use opposite adverbs, and this time add to your sentences using the word 'because', e.g. Today I walked slowly to the shops because I was tired after yesterday's party. Check your spelling in a dictionary. Do all your adverbs end in 'ly'?

WORD

1 Add 'ed' to: fill, smell, comfort, live, bare. Which final letters change when you add 'ed'? Check your answers in a dictionary. Write a rule to explain why.

2 Add 'ing' to: swing, change, snow, drive, print, manage. Check your answers in a dictionary. Which final letters change when you add 'ing'? Write a rule to explain why.

3 Many of our words have Greek suffixes, e.g. 'phobia' meaning 'fear'.
Find some more examples of words using these suffixes:

phobia   graph   ology   cracy

Making a Windmill

Instructions for making a windmill

You will need:
- ▼ a piece of thick paper cut out in a square
- ▼ some scissors
- ▼ a pin or two
- ▼ two beads
- ▼ a piece of thin stick.

(a)

(b)

(c)

(d)

(e)

(f)

(g)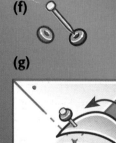

(h)

(a) Cut a 15 cm square of paper. Fold this from corner to corner and open out.

(b) Bend over and fold the other corner.

(c) Open out. Check that your paper square has creases like this one.

(d) Cut each corner on the crease and stop half-way. Turn the paper over pattern side down if you are using patterned wallpaper.

(e) With your pencil make a dot in the left-hand corner of each side. Make a pinhole through each dot and one through the centre.

(f) Put a small bead on the pin.

(g) Bend over, to the centre, one of the corners and put the pin through the hole.

(h) Bend over the next corner and push the pin through. Do the same with the other two corners and last of all put the pin through the centre hole. Slip the second bead on the pin and push the pin into the end of the stick.

TEXT

1 Which section did the writer put first?

2 Why is this an important feature when giving these kinds of instructions?
Could it be placed anywhere else in the passage? Why not?

3 Why did the writer use bullet points in front of items in the 'what you need' list?
How do they help the reader?

4 The instructions each have a different letter in front of them.
Why is this important for instructions?

5 Do you think the instructions are clear enough?
Which parts could you improve and how?

SENTENCE

1 Make a list of the verbs used in these instructions. What do you notice about them?

2 What tense are these verbs in?
You can check this for yourself by following this chart:

At this moment I …	Yesterday I …	Tomorrow I …
fold	folded	will fold

3 Change the instructions into the past tense. Write them starting, 'Yesterday, I made a windmill. I cut a small square of paper and folded this …'

4 Underline all the verbs which changed their spelling when the tense changed.
Write some rules about these changes.

WORD

1 The plural of 'windmill' is 'windmills'. What is the most common way of forming the plural of a noun? Write five examples from the instructions opposite, e.g. 'pin', 'pins'.

2 The plural of 'box' is 'boxes'. How do we form the plural of words ending in 'ch', 's', 'sh', 'ss' and 'x'? Write two examples of each. Use a dictionary.

3 The plural of 'lady' is 'ladies'. The plural of 'baby' is 'babies'. Look at the final two letters of these words. Can you make a rule for forming the plurals of words ending like this? Write five more examples.

4 Write the plurals of 'half', 'calf', 'shelf', 'self', 'wolf'. Use dictionaries to investigate this and find a rule.

5 What is the plural of 'scissors'? Is this word always plural?
Write two more words that are almost always used in the plural.

15

Story structure

Every story should have a beginning, a middle and an end.

> I'm freezing. He never lets me have any coal.

> A Merry Christmas, Uncle!

1 Continue the story of *A Christmas Carol* in the extract as a picture story. Start it like this and draw some more pictures of your own.

2 Do stories always have to follow this order? Write the story of the passage as a 'flashback', starting at the end:

'He should be boiled with his own pudding and buried with a stake of holly through his heart,' I said, but I wish I hadn't. It's all different now. I remember that day when I was in my counting house …

3 Carry on with the story from where the passage finishes in Unit 1.1. Use these questions to help: ▶

- ◆ Why does Scrooge act so nastily?
- ◆ Does he change?
- ◆ What happens to him?
- ◆ What is the story of his clerk?
- ◆ What happens to him?

Playscripts

4 Write *The Owl and the Pussy-Cat* as a play. Use all these features:

- ◆ write characters' names on the left
- ◆ start on a new line when they speak
- ◆ don't use speech marks
- ◆ don't use 'he said', etc.
- ◆ use stage directions for actions
- ◆ put stage directions in italics
- ◆ use prompts to actors in brackets

5 Imagine that you are visiting the home of Bilbo Baggins, the hobbit. Read the passage again and write about your visit as a play.

Giving instructions

6 Read Unit 1.5 again. What have you learned about writing clear instructions? Copy and complete the chart.

Instructions	Reason	Why?
have what you need first		
number the instructions		
follow a logical sequence		
use bullet points		
provide diagrams		
use clear, short sentences		

7 Here is a simple recipe, but it has got muddled up. Use what you have learned to write it out correctly again:

Recipe

Finally, eat it!

First, cut some bread.

How to make toast.

Then, select the cooking time on the dial of the toaster.

You need an electric toaster.

When the toast pops up, remove it.

Then insert the bread.

Next, butter the toast.

8 Writing instructions is easier if you use a pattern or format. Write some simple instructions, e.g. putting a disk into a computer. Use the format below to help you write some simple instructions:

You need...
First...
Then...
When...
After that...
Next...
Finally...

Story Planning Checklist

Type of story

What type of story do you want to write:

◆ adventure? mystery? animal? funny? other?

Setting

When will the story take place:

◆ in the present? in the past? in the future?
◆ Where will it take place? in a town? in a castle? in an imaginary place?

Characters

Who will the main characters be?

◆ Will they be human – people you know or made up?
◆ Will they be animals?
◆ What will the characters be like?

Plot

◆ How will the story begin?
◆ What sorts of things will happen in the story?
◆ How will the story end?
◆ Will it be happy or sad, mysterious or exciting?

How are you getting on with things in the chart? If you need extra practice, try the activities shown.

Grammar and punctuation	Adverbs qualifying verbs	1
	Person and tenses of verbs	2
	Commands (Imperatives)	3
	Dialogue	4
	Synonyms	5
Spelling, phonics and vocabulary	Spelling polysyllabic words	6
	Prefixes	7
	Suffixes	8
	Plurals	9

1 Copy these sentences. Find suitable adverbs.

a) To speak … is to whisper.

b) To jump … on one leg is to hop.

c) To eat … is to gulp.

d) To walk … is to dawdle.

e) To shout … is to scream.

2 Complete the chart in the present and the past tense.

Today I …	Yesterday I …	Today he …	Yesterday he …
hear	heard	hears	heard
am			
run			
have			
jump			
sit			

3 Change these sentences into commands (imperatives). Write the sentences.

e.g. 'May I take a sweet?' becomes 'Take a sweet.'

a) It is possible to switch off the TV.

b) Fred can pull the joystick of the computer game.

c) Would you care to drink your tea?

d) It is not easy to make a cake.

e) My teacher asked me to write out the spelling list.

4 Write this passage correctly. Some of the punctuation of speech is wrong.

Christmas a humbug, Uncle said Scrooge's nephew. You don't mean that, I'm sure? I do said Scrooge.

Merry Christmas! What right have you to be merry?

What reason have you to be merry? You're poor enough. Come then, returned the nephew gaily. What right have you to be dismal? What reason have you to be morose? You're rich enough?

5 Find synonyms for 'big'. Copy the sentences and put in the best word.

a) The warehouse was so … you could fit two planes in it.

b) Looking like a … finger in the sky, the office-block towered above us.

c) She ate and ate, week after week, until she was …

d) Saturday's football crowd packed out the stadium. It was …

6 *a)* Copy these words from *The Hobbit*. How many syllables do they contain? Sandy – 2 syllables e.g.

painted   comfortable   bathrooms   dining
asking   altogether   unexpected

b) Write them out, broken into syllables and underline any smaller words you can find inside the bigger words, e.g. san-dy. I can find the word <u>sand</u>.

7 Using a dictionary and a thesaurus, make words using each of these prefixes. Their meanings are given in brackets:

re (back) un (not) sub (under) mis (wrong) uni (one)

8 Use a thesaurus to find out more about ancient Greek suffixes, e.g. What does 'graphy' at the end of a word mean? what does 'ology' at the end of a word mean? What does 'phobia' at the end of a word mean? Find three examples of words using each of these suffixes.

9 Write the plurals of these nouns:

penny   class   knife   donkey   mouse   six
church duty   brush   piano

Handy hints for spelling

◆ Is the word spelt as it sounds? Does it contain any phonemes you already know?

◆ Does the word look right? Do you know any other words like it?

◆ Can you break the word into smaller parts? Which is the most difficult part of the word?

◆ Do you know what the word means?

◆ Have you used a word book or dictionary to help you?

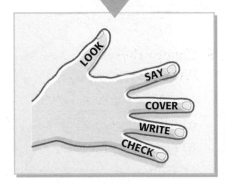

LOOK
SAY
COVER
WRITE
CHECK

Jim Hedgehog and the Lonesome Tower

Jim Hedgehog liked his music loud and he liked it heavy. He listened to Giant Squid and Crashing Boars and Really Disgusting Things from the Deep Swamp. He listened to Truly Rotten and Monstrous Midnight and Gravedigger's Express. He listened to Antimatter and Beyond the Galaxy and Spacewind and Black Hole. He was always on the lookout for new heavy metal groups.

One Saturday Jim went with his mother to the market. All up and down the street were stalls that sold fruit, vegetables, shirts, trousers, jackets, jumble, shoelaces, batteries, records, cassettes, umbrellas, Elastoplasts, and many other things.

While Mum was buying vegetables Jim went to the music stall. There was a stoat wearing dark glasses minding it. "Strange is my name and music's my game," he said. "If you don't see what you want, ask for it."

"Got any new heavy metal?" said Jim.

"Try this on your earholes," said Mr Strange. He handed Jim a cassette with a handwritten label.

"Is Lonesome Tower the album or the group?" said Jim.

"It's part of a building," said Mr Strange.

"What's the group?" said Jim.

"It's a thing," said Mr Strange.

"Why doesn't it say Itsa Thing on the cassette?" said Jim.

"Cheap cassette," said Mr Strange.

Jim listened to the beginning of the tape. It sounded like a hundred tomcats and a thousand bees in the middle of a hurricane. "That's not bad," he said.

"Hear any words?" said Mr Strange.

"Sure," said Jim. "Haven't you?"

"No, I haven't," said Mr Strange. "What do you hear?"

Russell Hoban

TEXT

1 What kind of music does Jim Hedgehog like?

2 Explain what you think of the names of the groups. Give your reasons.

3 Why do you think the author wanted to make you laugh at the beginning of this story?

4 How does the author make you interested in the mystery of the cassette? Give examples.

5 Use your own words to describe what the music is like when Jim listens to it.

6 What do you learn about Mr Strange? Use these questions to help:
   What does he look like? What does he wear? How does he act? What does he say?

7 Write a paragraph to describe the character of Mr Strange.

SENTENCE

1 Use connectives such as 'and', 'when', 'so', 'but', 'because' to make the passage below more interesting. You do not have to do this with every sentence.

Jim liked heavy metal music. His mum didn't. He bought the loud music. She was not pleased. She thought he was wasting his money. Jim and his mum went to the market. They met Mr Strange. He sold them a tape. The tape sounded strange. Jim took it home. He played it. The music was the same as his recorder music. Jim goes on a walk. It leads him to a haunted castle.

2 Now continue the story. Include some dialogue in it.

3 When you finish, compare it to the passage above. Say why it is more interesting.

WORD

1 In the passage, the writer only uses 'said' after each piece of speech. Choose five examples and write adverbs to describe how the words were said,
   e.g. 'What's the group?' said Jim, *enthusiastically*.

2 Sometimes the verb and an adverb can be replaced by just one verb, e.g. 'said quietly' could be replaced by 'whispered'. Take your examples from question 1.
   Find and write verbs to replace them.

3 Copy this chart and add five adverbs which you could use with each type of verb.

Type of verb	Adverbs
speed – e.g. to race	quickly
light – e.g. to shine	brightly

4 Most adverbs end in 'ly' but what happens with the following words?
   fast   hard   long   early   well

The Owl Service

"Roger's gone for a swim. You wanting company, are you?"

"Don't put yourself out for me," said Alison.

"Right," said Gwyn. "Cheerio."

He rode sideways down the banisters on his arms to the first floor landing.

"Gwyn!"

"Yes? What's the matter? You OK?"

"Quick!"

"You want a basin? You going to throw up, are you?"

"Gwyn!"

He ran back. Alison was kneeling on the bed.

"Listen," she said. "Can you hear that?"

"That what?"

"That noise in the ceiling. Listen."

The house was quiet. Mostyn Lewis-Jones was calling after the sheep on the mountain: and something was scratching in the ceiling above the bed.

"Mice," said Gwyn.

"Too loud," said Alison.

"Rats, then."

"No. Listen. It's something hard."

"They want their claws trimming."

"It's not rats," said Alison.

"It is rats. They're on the wood: that's why they're so loud."

"I heard it the first night I came," said Alison, "and every night since: a few minutes after I'm in bed."

"That's rats," said Gwyn. "As bold as you please."

"No," said Alison. "It's something trying to get out. The scratching's a bit louder each night. And today – it's the loudest yet – and it's not there all the time."

"They must be tired by now," said Gwyn.

"Today – it's been scratching when the pain's bad. Isn't that strange?"

"You're strange," said Gwyn. He stood on the bed, and rapped the ceiling. "You up there! Buzz off!"

The bed jangled as he fell, and landed hard, and sat gaping at Alison.

His knocks had been answered.

"Gwyn! Do it again!"

Gwyn stood up.

Knock, knock.

Scratch, scratch.

Knock.

Scratch.

Knock knock knock.

Scratch scratch scratch.

Knock – knock knock.

Scratch – scratch scratch.

Gwyn whistled. "Hey," he said.

Alan Garner

TEXT

1 What are the names of the three children in the story?

2 Find evidence to show that their house was not in the town.

3 What does Gwyn think is making the noise?

4 Why is Gwyn surprised when he knocks on the ceiling?

5 Read the final paragraph. Is this a good way to describe the noises? Why?

6 Show what you found out about the characters in the passage.
Use these questions to help:

How does Gwyn show he wants to be friends?

How does Alison show that she does not want to be friends?

How can you tell Gwyn has a sense of humour?

How does Alison prove that she thinks carefully about things?

SENTENCE

1 The author does not always name the speakers in this passage. How do you know who is speaking?

2 Copy the first three speeches. Circle the speech marks in red and the capital letters in blue. Underline the other punctuation in green. Write out a rule to explain each of these.

3 Check your rules against the next four or five lines of speech. Were you correct or do you have to change your rules for punctuating speech?

4 The author only uses the verb 'said' after speech. Find two better verbs for each time it is used, e.g. shouted, whispered. These must be suitable for *what* is being said and *how* it is being said.

WORD

1 This story deals with the supernatural. 'Super' is a Latin prefix meaning 'more than'. Use a dictionary to find three more words with this prefix.

2 Find out what the prefixes at the beginning of these words mean:

bilingual submerge malfunction exit advance thermometer

Give another example using the same prefix.

3 'In', 'im', and 'il' often make words negative, e.g. invisible. Find more examples of all three prefixes.

4 Use a dictionary. Find the meanings of these Greek and Latin prefixes:

tele aqua auto photo ultra micro

Give two examples of how each one is used.

A Football Report

Enfield Independent

Enfield use their Heads for Victory

Es reap rewards for set pieces

Bishop's Stortford 0
Enfield 2

(Ryman Isthmian Premier Div)

Skill in dead-ball situations proved the difference between the two sides on Saturday as the Es used their heads to secure a 2-0 victory over Stortford.

Second-half headed goals from a free kick and then a corner by Jason Tucker and Steve McGrath were enough to win the match in front of Stortford's biggest crowd of the season.

In a surprise change for the Es, young goalkeeper Andy Hall was dropped with new recruit from Staines Tony Wells taking his place.

In the first half there was little sight of goalmouth chances, or attractive football, as both teams struggled to cope with a slippery pitch.

Further changes were forced on the Es early on. Eric Young had to be substituted after only five minutes when he crashed to the ground following a defensive clearance. Matt Edwards replaced him.

And on 13 minutes manager Graham Westley decided to replace Lee Endersby, who was struggling on the wing, with Venables.

Until Edwards blasted a 30-yard drive over the Stortford crossbar the biggest drama was the booking of Stortford's Tony Comerford for a bad tackle.

The Es went into the break looking the better side but failed to break through until the 57th minute when a free kick by Deadman was lofted into the Stortford area.

Paul Moran headed the kick back across goal and Tucker rose at the far post to head it past keeper Gavin King.

Soon after King palmed a fierce shot from Steve Darlington round the post.

Leroy May and Dave Venables for the Es followed Comerford into the referee's notebook as both teams went in hard. They were then joined by Stortford's Cove and Wardley.

On 79 minutes Es wrapped the game up with a goal in similar fashion. This time Deadman curved in a corner, Moran kept it in the air with a clever back header and Steve McGrath was waiting to nod the ball into the net.

TEXT

1 Which team were Enfield Town playing? What was the score?

2 When were the two goals scored in the match? Who scored them?

3 What words tell you that the reporter thought the match was quite boring in the first half?

4 Write down the words that start each paragraph. Some of these words connect one paragraph to another, e.g. Soon after. They are called connectives. Which other words in your list do the same thing?

5 Find examples from the passage of these features of news reports:

- **short paragraphs**   • **abbreviations**
- **opening summarises story**
- **follows events stage by stage**
- **uses headlines**

SENTENCE

1 Write down the verb from paragraph five which describes Eric Young's fall. Why did the writer think his choice was a better verb to use than 'fell'?

2 Use a thesaurus to write down another two verbs that the writer could have used.

3 Write down the verb from paragraph seven which describes Edwards scoring a goal. Why did the writer think his choice was a better verb to use than 'kick'?

4 Find another two verbs that the writer could have used.

5 Write some sentences of your own. Use the new words you have found in the thesaurus.

WORD

1 Explain what these football expressions mean:

- **dead-ball situation**
- **followed Comerford into the referee's notebook**
- **went into the break**

2 Find evidence to show that you have to know a lot about football to be able to understand the language of this report.

3 Write down two clichés in the report. Explain what they mean in your own words.

4 Use a dictionary or thesaurus. Find two different synonyms which could replace each adjective in these descriptions:

a *big* crowd   *attractive* football   *slippery* pitch

5 Find the descriptions in question 4 in the passage and say how your new words change the meaning.

The Borrowers

Pod did not speak until they reached the sitting-room. Nor did he look at her. She had had to scramble after him as best she might. He had ignored her efforts to help him shut the gates, but once, when she tripped, he had waited until she had got up again, watching her, it seemed, almost without interest while she brushed the dust off her knees.

Supper was laid and the ironing put away and Homily came running in from the kitchen, surprised to see them together.

Pod threw down his borrowing-bag. He stared at his wife.

"What's the matter?" faltered Homily, looking from one to the other.

"She was in the night-nursery," said Pod quietly, "talking to that boy!"

Homily moved forward, her hands clasped tremblingly against her apron, her startled eyes flicking swiftly to and fro. "Oh, no –" she breathed.

Pod sat down. He ran a tired hand over his eyes and forehead; his face looked heavy like a piece of dough. "Now what?" he said.

Homily stood quite still; she stood bowed over her clasped hands and stared at Arrietty. "Oh, you never – " she whispered.

"They are frightened," Arrietty realized; "they are not angry at all – they are very, very frightened." She moved forward. "It's all right –" she began.

Homily sat down suddenly on the cotton-reel; she had begun to tremble. "Oh," she said, "whatever shall we do?" She began to rock herself, very slightly, to and fro.

"Oh, mother, don't!" pleaded Arrietty. "It isn't so bad as that. It really isn't." She felt up the front of her jersey; at first she could not find the letter – it had slid round her side to the back – but at last she drew it out, very crumpled. "Look," she said, "here's a letter from Uncle Hendreary. I wrote to him and the boy took the letter – "

"You wrote to him!" cried Homily in a kind of suppressed shriek. "Oh," she moaned, and closed her eyes, "whatever next! Whatever shall we do?" and she fanned herself limply with her bony hand.

"Get your mother a drink of water, Arrietty," said Pod sharply. Arrietty brought it in a sawn-off hazel shell – it had been sawn off at the pointed end and was shaped like a brandy glass.

Mary Norton

TEXT

1 What are the names of the three characters?

2 Draw and label a family tree using evidence from the passage. Draw the family tree like this:

Mother —— Father

Daughter

3 They are Borrowers. What does Pod carry to prove this?

4 Write down some evidence that proves that Pod and Homily are both frightened.

5 What has Arrietty done to make them so frightened?

6 What two pieces of evidence can you find to prove that the Borrowers are tiny people?

7 Explain how these examples help to make you feel what it could be like to be so small.

SENTENCE

1 Find and write examples in the passage of verbs using each of these forms:

I you he she it we they

2 Write down examples from the passage of verbs used in different tenses. Sort them into a chart, like this:

Present tense	Past tense	Future tense
	They reached	Whatever shall we do?

3 In your examples, change some of these tenses, e.g. past instead of future. Say how it changes the meaning of each sentence.

4 Write five things that the Borrowers say in reported *not* direct speech, e.g. Homily asked what the matter was.

WORD

1 Write these words from the passage and divide them into syllables:

sitting (2) watching (2) running (2) borrowing (3)

2 *a)* What suffix do they all have in common? *b)* Write down the root in each word.
c) Underline where any spelling changes have happened when the suffix was added.

3 Write these words from the passage and divide them into syllables:

frightened whispered reacted clasped realized crumpled pointed shaped

4 *a)* What suffix do they all have in common? *b)* Write down the root in each word.
c) Underline where any spelling changes happened when the suffix was added.

5 What happens when you add 'ing' or 'ed' to words ending in a vowel, e.g. shape? Make up a rule and find five more examples to prove your rule.

How Do I Programme a Video Recorder?

In this chapter you will learn how to programme your set. It switches itself on automatically, records the TV programme you want and then automatically switches itself off again.

What information does the set need?

The set needs the following information for every programmed recording:

- the date on which the recording is to be made
- the programme number for the TV channel
- the start time of the recording
- the stop time of the recording

The set stores all the information necessary for a recording in what is known as a TIMER block. And it does that for up to one month in advance.

Your set can store up to 6 of these TIMER blocks. Please note that the timing of the TIMER blocks must not overlap. The video recorder must first finish one TIMER block before starting the next block.

Programming on the set

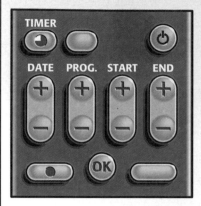

You can enter and store data in the set for six recordings.

The TV screen will show all the data simultaneously.

Use the four +/− buttons on the remote control to enter the data.

The data will be stored in the set in the next free TIMER block.

Make sure you have not loaded a cassette with erase protection.

1 Switch on the set. Press the TIMER button on the remote control.

A free TIMER block will appear on the TV screen. You will see the current data for the date, programme number, start time and stop time. Change the data in any sequence you choose:

- Set the date of the recording with the DATE +/− button.
- Set the programme number with the PROG. +/− button.
- Set the start time with the START +/− button.
- Set the stop time with the END +/− button.

2 Have you set all the data correctly? Now press the OK button on the remote control.

If you want to finish, press the CLEAR button.

Programming is now complete. The data has been stored in a TIMER block. The TIMER lamp on the front of the set lights up when one or more of the TIMER blocks are occupied.

TEXT

1 In the first paragraph, what three things are we told that the video recorder does?

2 How many pieces of information does the set need for a programmed recording?

3 Copy these statements. Say if they are true or false. Give reasons:

a) The TV screen will show all data at the same time.   b) You cannot change the data in any sequence.   c) You press the clear button to finish.   d) The timer lamp on the TV will light up when the tape is out.

4 Here are six features of written instructions. Find evidence for each feature in the passage:

- **introduction for the reader**   ● **instructions in the right order**   ● **uses numbers**
- **uses bullet points**   ● **uses commands**   ● **uses technical words**

SENTENCE

1 Read through the instructions again. Write down all the verbs you can find.

2 Now write them in three columns to sort out their tenses: past, present and future.

3 What do you notice? Why do you think most instructions are written in this tense?

4 Find four verbs that are in the imperative – giving you orders, e.g. (you) go. Why do you find these so often in instructions and not in other kinds of writing?

5 Find the adverbs in the passage that go with:

- **switches on**   ● **show the data**   ● **set the data**

WORD

1 How many words can you make by adding to the beginning of these root words: tend, pend, pand, port? e.g. intend, pretend.

2 You can make a noun from a verb by adding 'tion', e.g. to inform – information. Notice that the letter 'a' has to be added here to make the word easier to say. Turn these verbs into nouns by adding 'tion' and make any other changes that are necessary:

create   perfect   inspect   examine   compete

Underline the words where the spelling changes.

3 How many words can you make from the root word 'satisfy' by adding a prefix and changing the ending, e.g. unsatisfying?

4 Use a thesaurus or dictionary. How many words can you make using these Latin or Greek roots? (Hint: In some words, only a part of the root is used, e.g. verbal.)

scriptus = written   **verbum = a word**   **manus = a hand**

Newspaper reports

Read this short newspaper article and its features:

headline

It's chips for computer thief

topic sentence

short paragraph that explains topic sentence

use of simple description

The twenty computer chips stolen from a west London primary school last week were posted immediately outside the school, a jury heard yesterday.

The two thieves broke into the school in the early hours of the morning, and stole the silicon chips. Immediately outside the school, they got rid of the evidence by posting them to a friend, Prosecutor Peter Smith told the Old Bailey.

Blond-haired Mr Smith alleged that 18 year old self-employed locksmith Fred Bloggs knew the computers would be in the school. Mr Bloggs later told the police: 'I don't know nothing about no computer chips. I've been framed.'

Fastest growing crime

Mr Smith also told the jury that the theft of computer chips was the fastest growing crime in the area. The goods were easy to dispose of and could be sold at a great profit.

'It is even worse in that he was depriving poor children of a valuable educational experience.' Bloggs was sentenced to a year's community service. It was chips for him.

sub-headings as key words

A combination of direct and reported speech

1 Write your own silly, shocking classroom news story using the same sort of features such as headings, topic sentences etc.

Ideas for your shocking articles:

Boy falls over in playground!

Pencil falls from desk!

Bell rings for end of lesson!

2 Read the passage from *The Borrowers* again. Write a newspaper article about the discovery of the Borrowers by the boy.

Describing characters

3 You can describe what characters look like. Imagine that Mr Strange from *Jim Hedgehog and the Lonesome Tower* was missing and that you were the last person to see him. Write a description of him for the police and make a wanted poster. Think about: body build, height, shape of face, shape of nose, colour of eyes, any special features.

4 Read the passage from *The Owl Service* again. Continue the story. Give your reader a strong sense of the two characters through what they say and *do*. It is also your chance to describe what they look like more carefully.

Point of view

5 Write what the world would look and feel like from the point of view of the Borrowers. What is it like being so small? What do ordinary objects look like to them? What are they afraid of? What do they eat?

6 Imagine you had to sell the home of the Borrowers. Write a short description which aims to sell it. You will need to persuade your reader that it is very special. Make notes about its features in a chart like this:

Features:

Shape:

Colour:

Writing steps

1 Planning

What will your piece of writing be about?

Use the Story Planning Checklist in Writing Focus 1.1.

Talk about your ideas with others.

2 Drafting

Write the first draft of your ideas in rough.

Use a word processor or paper.

3 Reviewing

Read your work.

Talk about it with someone else.

Make changes. Cross out parts, change or add more words and sentences.

Use a thesaurus.

4 Editing

Check through your work for small mistakes in spelling and punctuation.

Use a dictionary.

Ask someone else to check your work, too.

5 Publishing

How do you want your work published?

As a book? On paper?

Use a computer to help you.

Think about illustration.

Publish your work and be proud of it!

How are you getting on with things in the chart?

If you need extra practice, try the activities shown.

Grammar and punctuation	Adverbs qualifying verbs	1
	Verb tenses	2
	Dialogue verbs	3
	Making complex sentences	4
	Punctuation of speech	5
	Reported speech	6
Spelling, phonics and vocabulary	Plurals	7
	Prefixes and suffixes	8
	Synonyms	9
	Roots of words and wordbuilding	10

1 Match the pairs of nouns and verbs. Find a suitable adverb and write a sentence, e.g. dog matches with bark: The dog barked loudly in the night.

| **noun** | bells | horns | keys | dog | fire | lion |
| **verb** | blare | ring | roar | crackle | jingle | bark |

2 *a)* Write four sentences about what the weather *was* like yesterday, using the past tense. Start: Yesterday the weather *was* …

   b) Now write four sentences about what the weather *will be* like tomorrow, using the future tense. Start: Tomorrow, the weather *will be* …

3 Copy these sentences and put in a better verb than 'said'.

   a) "Ouch!" … Fred as he dropped the box on his foot.

   b) "It's so boring," … Ranjit. "We never go anywhere".

   c) "Help! Please help me," he … from the hole beneath the ground.

   d) I … the answer to the teacher, because felt shy.

4 Write six sentences about a controversial subject, e.g. should fox-hunting be banned? Use the connecting words in the box at the beginning of each new idea.

I think fox hunting is cruel because …

Indeed …

However…

For example …

Therefore …

To conclude …

5 Write this passage correctly. Some of the punctuation of speech is wrong.

Is Lonesome Tower the album or the group? said Jim. It's part of a building, said Mr Strange.

What's the group? said Jim. It's a thing, said Mr Strange. Why doesn't it say Itsa Thing on the cassette? said Jim. Cheap cassette said Mr Strange.

6 Write these speeches as reported speech:

Miss Smith: I do not want to inhale the smoke of other people. It is unhealthy.

Doctor: A person who smokes every day will endanger their health.

Tracy: I don't like being in a room with smokers. My clothes smell.

Wayne: There is nothing wrong with smoking. I am free to do what I like.

7 Write the plurals of the following nouns:
ash   glass   fireman   baby   country   dwarf   scissors

8 The suffix 'ible' or 'able' means 'able to be'. Write what the following words mean. Write sentences to show you can use them properly:
portable   visible   edible   understandable

9 *a)* These words are all synonyms for 'touch':
prod   knead   grip   pinch   press   massage   pat

Find out what they mean and write them in sentences to show their meaning.

b) Find five synonyms for 'smell'. Explain their different meanings in sentences.

10 Look at these words:
flexible   spreadable   traceable   legible   drinkable

a) Which ones can you make negative by adding 'in' or 'un' before them?

b) Decide what the root of each word is. To which words can you add 'ing'? To which words can you add 'ility'? Does the spelling change when you word build?

- Is the word spelt as it sounds? Does it contain any phonemes you already know?

- Does the word look right? Do you know any other words like it?

- Can you break the word into smaller parts? Which is the most difficult part of the word?

- Do you know what the word means?

- Have you used a word book or dictionary to help you?

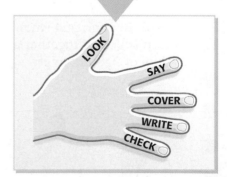

LOOK   SAY   COVER   WRITE   CHECK

Jason and the Golden Fleece

Jason's father, a Greek king, has been killed by Pelias, Jason's evil brother. After Pelias takes over the kingdom, Jason is sent out of the country to live with Chiron, a wise centaur – half man and half horse. Chiron looks after Jason for many years and teaches him how to be strong, how to fight and how to be a leader.

When Jason was old enough, he returned to claim his throne, but his clever brother had thought of a plan to get rid of him. Pelias would not let Jason become king until he had found the Golden Fleece – a sheepskin made of pure gold. The Fleece was guarded by a huge snake and so was impossible to steal. To win his prize, Jason had to travel to Colchis, so he had a boat built by a man called Argos. The boat was called the Argo and when Jason collected together a group of fighters to go with him on the quest, they were named Argonauts after their fine ship.

He and his crew had many heroic adventures on the way to Colchis. They were attacked by enormous six-armed monsters, they captured the harpies – cruel, winged monsters, escaped the furies of clashing rocks in the Greek seas, and were attacked by huge birds with bronze feathers. But all the time they were being protected by the Goddess Hera because Jason had helped her earlier in his life.

Eventually they arrived in Colchis, but the king there did not want to let go of the Golden Fleece. He pretended to be welcoming but he set Jason three tasks to show that he was fit to be the owner of the precious Fleece. Jason would not have succeeded in these if it had not been for the king's daughter, Medea, who had fallen in love with him.

Jason's tasks were to attach two fierce bulls to a plough, to sow a field with seed and then gather in the crop that grew. Medea warned him that he was being tricked. The bulls her father would give him breathed fire, the seeds he had to sow were magical dragon's teeth and the crop that would grow would be an army of soldiers, who would kill him. But what could he do?

Medea gave him magic ointment. This would prevent him being burned by the bulls. He also carried a shiny shield so that the fire was reflected back at the bulls. The dragons' teeth would burn him so he wore gloves and he could fight the soldiers by himself because he was so strong.

TEXT

1 *a)* Who looked after Jason when he was a child? *b)* Why was he a strange choice? *c)* What did he teach Jason?

2 Explain why Jason's warriors were called the 'Argonauts'.

3 Give three examples of adventures that the Argonauts had on their way to Colchis.

4 *a)* What were the three tasks given to Jason? *b)* Explain how he was tricked.

5 *a)* Show how he solved his three problems. *b)* Who helped him, and why?

6 Here are five features of legends. Find examples from the passage to illustrate them.

- **story takes place in the olden days**   ● **story has monsters**   ● **story has strong heroes**
- **there are battles or fights**   ● **good wins in the end**

SENTENCE

1 Which of these words would you use to describe *a)* someone you liked and *b)* someone you did not like? Say why.

**graceful   puny   elegant   dainty   uncouth
handsome   scrawny   gloomy   cheerful   infantile**

2 *a)* What two adjectives are used to describe Jason's brother?
b) Describe how they make you feel about him.
c) If the author had wanted you to feel the opposite, what words might he have used?

3 Find the evidence to prove that Jason is: brave, heroic, intelligent and strong.

4 Use these four pieces of information to write a paragraph which describes Jason. How would you twist the information to make him sound not so heroic?

WORD

1 Write out these sentences using the correct form and spelling of the words.

a) (There/their/they're) bikes were stolen yesterday.

b) "Never mind (who's/whose) bikes they (where/we're/were)," said the teacher, "I want to know if (there/they're/their insured.)"

c) "(Its/it's) no good thinking of that now," said mum. "(There's/theirs) no excuse."

2 Write your own sentences using these pronouns:

them mine hers its yours theirs whose me

3 Write some rules for the class to explain when you use:

- **there, their or they're**   ● **where, were and we're**   ● **its and it's**   ● **whose and who's**

The Story of Osiris

Seth believed that he should be king, because he was the strongest of the children of Nout. He was furious that both his sisters loved Osiris more than they did him. In his heart Seth plotted to kill Osiris and become king.

Osiris often walked through Egypt to see that everything was going well in his kingdom. Seth followed him. One day he caught Osiris alone on the river bank. Seth spat fury at his brother: the strong arm of Seth seized Osiris. Seth struck down his brother.

Some say that Seth held Osiris under the Nile until he drowned. Others say that Seth took the form of a wild bull and trampled Osiris to death. Even that was not enough for Seth. He tore the body of his brother apart and scattered the pieces. Seth wanted to make sure that even the magic of Isis could not bring Osiris back to life.

When Osiris didn't return to the palace, Isis knew that something terrible had happened. She and her sister Nephthys searched the deserts and the marshes and the river valley. On the bank of the Nile, Isis found the head of Osiris. It took twelve days to gather all the pieces of the body together.

In despair, Isis called for the jackal god, Anubis, to help her: he is the deadly guardian of all graveyards.

Anubis laid the mangled body of Osiris on a bed. Isis and Anubis worked together to make the body whole again. Then Anubis cut open the stomach of Osiris with a flint knife. He reached inside and drew out the soft organs. He put the lungs and the liver, the stomach and the intestines of Osiris into four jars. Anubis washed the body with wine and covered it with natron salts to preserve it.

After forty days the skin was dried out by the salt. Anubis washed away the salt with Nile water. He packed the stomach with frankincense and myrrh and sewed up the wound. Anubis wrapped the head and limbs and torso in fine linen bandages.

Geraldine Harris

T E X T

1 Why did Seth think he should be king? Which country did Seth want to be king of?

2 Which river was Osiris murdered beside?

3 What were the names of the four children of the goddess Nout?

4 Write a list to explain all the stages the gods and goddesses went through to make Osiris a mummy.

5 Myths have certain features. Find some evidence of each of these features from the passage:

- **story about gods and goddesses**
- **tells of events with magic happenings**
- **involves evil doings by a god**
- **takes place in a different culture**
- **takes place a long time ago**
- **tries to explain the reason for**
- **something important through the story**

S E N T E N C E

1 Write out these sentences. Punctuate them correctly with commas.

a) Anubis cut open the stomach drew out the soft organs put them in jars and preserved the body.

b) On his visit to the far east he visited Sri Lanka Indonesia Singapore Thailand and Malaysia.

c) "Are you all ready too" she said. "Right off we go."

2 If we do not use commas correctly, it can cause confusion.
Read this sentence:

The holiday was fun: there was the bike, the computer, the tree house, my cousin, Ranjit, my friend, Ros, the teacher's daughter.

Count up. How many things and people made the holiday fun?

3 Write out the sentence, using commas differently, so you count up a different number.

W O R D

1 Write three words ending in 'll' to rhyme with each of these: bull, ball, bell, fill.

2 How many syllables do these words have? Write a rule for spelling simple words ending in 'll'.

3 Add 'full' to these words: spoon, hate, thank, play, cheer, e.g. hope → hopeful. Check in a dictionary.

4 Try the same with these words: skill, awe, beauty. Does anything strange happen?

5 How many syllables do the words you made have? Write a rule for spelling words when 'full' is used as a suffix, making longer words.

The Pied Piper of Hamelin

The Pied Piper removed all the rats of Hamelin. He made them follow him by playing his magic flute. He then led them to the river where they drowned. The Town Council did not pay him, as promised, for doing this. Now he takes his revenge.

Once more he stept into the street;
    And to his lips again
Laid his long pipe of smooth straight cane;
    And ere he blew three notes (such sweet
Soft notes as yet musician's cunning
    Never gave the enraptured air)
There was a rustling that seem'd like a bustling
Of merry crowds justling at pitching and hustling,
Small feet were pattering, wooden shoes clattering,
Little hands clapping, and little tongues chattering,
And, like fowls in a farm-yard when barley
    is scattering,
Out came the children running.
All the little boys and girls,
With rosy cheeks and flaxen curls,
And sparkling eyes and teeth like pearls,
Tripping and skipping, ran merrily after
The wonderful music with shouting and laughter.

The Mayor was dumb, and the Council stood
As if they were changed into blocks of wood,
Unable to move a step, or cry
To the children merrily skipping by –
And could only follow with the eye
That joyous crowd at the Piper's back.
But how the Mayor was on the rack,
And the wretched Council's bosoms beat,
As the Piper turn'd from the High Street
To where the Weser roll'd its waters
Right in the way of their sons and daughters!
However, he turned from south to west,
And to Koppelberg Hill his steps address'd,
And after him the children press'd;
Great was the joy in every breast.

Robert Browning

TEXT

1 *a)* What is the Piper's flute made from? *b)* How many notes did he play on it before the children appeared?

2 Write down three words in the poem that tell you that the children wanted to follow the Piper and were not being forced.

3 *a)* Read carefully the description of the 'little boys and girls', then write down four adjectives used to describe them, e.g. little.
   b) Do you feel sorry for the children?
   c) Do you feel sad that the Piper is taking them away?

4 Write down two verbs the poet uses when describing the children that give you the impression that they are very happy in what they are doing.

5 How can you tell from the words he has chosen, that the poet does not want you to like the council in the last part of the poem? Give reasons.

SENTENCE

1 Write out the present tense of the verb 'to be':
   I … **you** … **he/she/it** … **we**…
   you (all) … **they** …

2 Look in the poem to find out if these sentences are correct:
   a) The Mayor were dumb …
   b) As if they were changed …
   Explain your answers.

3 Write out these sentences. Put in the correct form of the verb 'to be'.
   a) The answer to the problem … more classrooms.
   b) The football results … out today.
   c) Everybody … very happy with the new England colours.
   d) The crew of the ship … working very hard.
   e) The police … not very happy with your behaviour.

4 Go back and check your answers. Ask yourself: "Am I talking about one or more than one subject?"

WORD

1 Write down five words from the poem that end in 'ing'. Write the root of the word, e.g. chattering – chatter is the root word.

2 Say if the root word changed its spelling when the 'ing' was added or whether it stayed the same.

3 Add 'ed' and 'ing' to the following verbs:
   hum beg skip stop pin tap

4 Write a rule for spelling these verbs when adding 'ed' and 'ing'.

5 Now do the same using these verbs:
   pedal kidnap worship travel begin
   Does the same thing happen?

The Diver

I put on my aqua-lung and plunge,
Exploring, like a ship with a glass keel,
The secrets of the deep. Along my lazy road
On and on I steal —
Over waving bushes which at a touch explode
Into shrimps, then closing rock to the tune of the tide;
Over crabs that vanish in puffs of sand.
Look, a string of pearls bubbling at my side
Breaks in my hand —
Those pearls were my breath! ... Does that hollow hide
Some old Armada wreck in seaweed furled,
Crusted with barnacles, her cannon rusted,
The great San Philip? What bullion in her hold?
Pieces of eight, silver crowns, and bars of solid gold?

I shall never know. Too soon the clasping cold
Fastens on flesh and limb
And pulls me to the surface. Shivering, back I swim
To the beach, the noisy crowds, the ordinary world.

Ian Serraillier

TEXT

1 Where is the poet exploring? How do you know?

2 *a)* Write down three living things the poet finds in this mysterious place.
   b) What does he say about them?

3 Describe what the poet imagines to be in the hollow. What kinds of things does he imagine could be inside this?

4 Why does the poet have to stop his adventure?

5 How is the world on the surface different from the world where he has just been?

6 Write down details about where the diver is, using this chart:

Place	Words to describe	Picture they give me
wreck	cannons rusted	old, dark, mysterious

SENTENCE

1 Read the poem again. What tense is the poem written in?
   Find three examples to prove you are correct.

2 Write out these sentences. Choose the correct verb in the brackets:

   a) The two cats (was/were) asleep. *b)* I (has/had) a difficult job to keep them quiet.

   c) I (see/saw) them when they came back. *d)* I am sure they (have/had) eaten already
   e) I (did/done) my homework quickly so I (can/could) play with them.
   f) They (lives/live) in my bedroom.

3 *a)* What tense are these sentences written in? *b)* Write out the sentences using another tense. What changes do you notice? *c)* Do the sentences still make sense? Give your reasons.

WORD

1 *a)* Say which of these words are sound words found in comics: slurp, biff, thwack, missed, jumped, woof. *b)* What kinds of sounds are they describing?

2 Write sentences using these sound (onomatopoeic) words in the past tense, e.g. pop: The cork popped out of the bottle.
   splash bang smack sizzle plop

3 Use these onomatopoeic words in sentences to write a piece of description, full of sounds:
   growl purr moo crunch squelch

4 What sort of sound words might be best to describe the following?
   a) a balloon bursting *b)* a glass dropping on a pavement *c)* someone falling in a river

Metals

Metal products are an essential part of our lives. For example, they can form the framework of Blackpool Tower or may be delicately formed into the hands on the café clock.

Most of the metals we use begin their lives in the earth as an ore. An ore is a mixture of metal and waste material. In order to extract the metal the waste material has to be removed.

When we make toffee the ingredients are mixed together and are heated in a pan. Eventually the mixture turns into a liquid which can be poured into a tray or moulds to cool. Metals can be cooked in a similar way. The process of extracting the metal from the ore is known as smelting.

If we melt two or more metals together we can form a new material. This material is called an alloy.

Copper and zinc are two soft metals. By melting them together they make an alloy called brass. Brass is harder and springier than either copper or zinc.

Metals can be divided into two groups which are called ferrous and non-ferrous metals.

Ferrous metals contain iron. Steel is a ferrous metal because it contains iron and carbon.

Non-ferrous metals do not contain any iron. Aluminium, copper, gold, lead, silver, tin and zinc are examples of non-ferrous metals.

From Looking at Materials *by Peter Stokes*

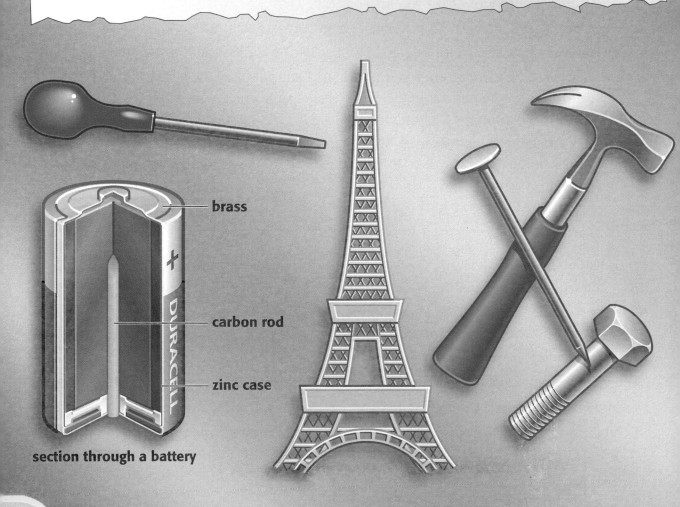

brass

carbon rod

zinc case

section through a battery

TEXT

1 Where do most metals we use come from at the very beginning?

2 What is the process of extracting metal from ore called?

3 *a)* What is an alloy? *b)* What is the point of making an alloy from copper and zinc?
c) Why is steel an alloy? Give reasons.

4 Look at the diagram of the battery. Copy these sentences.
Give reasons why they are true or false.

a) It is made completely from alloys. *b)* It is made using one non-ferrous metal.
c) A battery is made from copper, zinc and carbon.

5 Find examples from the passage to show these features of 'writing which aims
to explain something':

- **uses technical words**   • **uses 'we' or 'our', even though the writer does not know you**
- **helps you understand technical words** • **makes use of charts and diagrams**
- **uses words like 'when' and 'if' to suggest what might happen**

SENTENCE

1 Write down three common nouns and one proper noun from paragraph 1.

2 Write down five abstract nouns that are qualities you admire in people, e.g. honesty.
Write them in sentences to show you understand what they mean.

3 Make a list of *a)* ten proper nouns beginning with the first letter of your name
b) ten animals or birds beginning with the second letter of your name
c) an abstract noun beginning with the third letter of your name.

WORD

1 For each of these words, write down a word that sounds the same but has
a different spelling: **tale stare fur sore course write isle stationery**

2 Now find out what all the words mean. Write down the differences in meaning.

3 The passage talks about 'steel' and 'ore'. Use a dictionary and write down their
meanings. Find a homophone for each one and write down their definitions, too.

4 Copy this chart. The words in the first column have three possible spellings. Match them
with words in the second column and write another homophone in the third column.

poor	for	fore
two	too	
four	pour	

Using the idea in a poem for other kinds of writing

1 Think about what happens in the story of the *Pied Piper of Hamelin*. It is a very shocking story and if it happened today it would make the headlines of a newspaper. Write the story as a newspaper article. Remember to:

◆ write a headline, e.g. MYSTERIOUS PIPER STEALS CHILDREN

◆ think of a strong opening sentence to summarise the story

◆ tell what happened in stages using subheadings

◆ interview people, e.g. the Piper, the Mayor, the children, to find out why they acted as they did

◆ use the correct tenses and language for a newspaper article – this is not just telling a story, it is reporting the story for a purpose.

2 Imagine you were one of the children who followed the Piper and disappeared. Tell your story.
   ◆ Why did you follow him?
   ◆ Where did he take you?
   ◆ What was it like there?
   ◆ Did you miss your home?
   ◆ Did you ever come back? How?

3 Read Unit 2.4 again. Imagine that the diver really finds the ship he describes under the sea.

   ◆ How does he find it?

   ◆ What is it like?

   ◆ What is inside it?

   ◆ Is there anything mysterious about it?

Making notes in various ways

4 *a)* Read Unit 2.5 again. Write subheadings to sum up what a paragraph or section is about, e.g. paragraph 1 could be about 'Why metal is essential to us'.

   b) Now only use your notes and do not look back at the passage to write a short descriptive piece (no more than a paragraph or two) about metals.

5 Follow the pattern of Unit 2.5, and write a similar information passage about wood. Use the same kinds of subheadings as you have already written and follow their order.

Writing your own versions of legend and myths

6 Read Unit 2.1 again. The story of Jason stops before we know what really happens. Continue the story until the end.

◆ What happens when he faces his three challenges?

◆ Does the king find out that Medea has helped him?

◆ How does he get the Golden Fleece from the deadly snake?

◆ Does it all end happily ever after?

7 Read Unit 2.2 again. Imagine you are being asked to make a film of this extract. Produce some storyboards to show the film crew what the film will comprise of.

You will have to:

◆ break down the story into small parts, step by step

◆ make sure the parts of the story follow in order

◆ draw a picture for each of the separate parts

◆ write notes about what is happening in each scene

◆ suggest ideas for sound effects and script

◆ say what costumes and props you will need.

8 Write your own version of a traditional fairy story, but change one part to make the outcome different, e.g. what about if there was a Cinderfella and a Princess Charming? What if Goldilocks was a really nasty character? What if Superwoman became a Fairy Godmother?

Reviewing your writing

Firstly:

Does your piece of writing make sense?
Is there anything you cannot understand?

Generally:

Does it have: a beginning? a middle? an end?
Are all the parts in an order that makes sense?
Do you need to move parts around?
Is this the time to add anything new?
Have you missed out anything really important?

The contents:

Is there enough to interest your reader?
Are there any boring parts?
How can you make these more interesting?
Can you miss them out?

People:

Are any characters in your writing described in enough detail?
Have you described how they: look, act, feel, think?

Places:

Are the places in your writing described in enough detail?

Now:

You are ready to edit your writing.

How are you getting on with things in the chart? If you need extra practice try the activities shown.

Grammar and punctuation	Nouns	1
	Adapting writing for different audiences	2
	Confusions over pronouns	3
	Agreement – noun and verb	4
	Agreement – tense and subject	5
	Commas	6
Spelling, phonics and vocabulary	Consonants – 'll' and 'l'	7
	Consonants – adding 'ing' and 'ed'	8
	Homophones	9
	Onomatopoeia	10

1 *a)* Write out these expressions adding a correct noun:

a herd of …   a bouquet of …   a flock of …   a shoal of …   a swarm of …

b) Write the names of three of each of:

a) mountain ranges   b) countries
c) months of the year   d) girls' names.

What sort of nouns are these?

2 *a)* These words are to do with feelings. Imagine you were going to write about some people you liked or disliked, which words would you use for them?

sensible   irritating   annoying enthusiastic   pleasant   joyful despairing   depressing   sympathetic jealous   generous   energetic

b) Put the words in sentences to show you know what they mean.

3 *a)* Say why there is an apostrophe in:

they're   it's   you're   who's

Write sentences using the words to show you know what they mean.

b) Use these words which do not need apostrophes in sentences to show you know what they mean:

its   yours   theirs   whose.

4 Write out the sentences. Put in the correct form of the verb 'to be' – *is* or *are*. Give your reasons.

a) Emma, with her parents, brother and dog, … going to Brighton.

b) The class… not ready to leave.

c) Everyone… looking forward to to the weekend.

d) She is one of those people who… never bothered by the cold.

5 Write out the sentences. Choose the correct verb from the brackets. Give reasons for your choice.

a) The supermarket (have/has) a special offer on cat food.

b) We should not have (give/given) so much to them.

c) There (are/is) no tins left.

d) They (done/did) their best to eat it all.

6 Write out these sentences putting in commas to show pauses:

a) To mend the puncture you need a jack a wheel brace a spare tyre and a lot of patience!

b) The rain poured down the window but she could still see the buses the cars all the shoppers and at last her friend Sarah.

7 Add 'ful' to these words. Check your spelling in a dictionary:

tear   spite   cheer   spoon   hand

Say if the original word changes.

Find three exceptions to what you notice.

8 *a)* Add 'ing' to each word.

spit   manage   grow   begin   change

Check your spelling in a dictionary.

b) Say if the original word changes spelling.

9 *a)* Write sentences to show the differences in meaning between these homophones: know/no   new/knew.

b) Use a dictionary to find homophones for:

choose   throne   eight   beat   site   break

10 What sounds are these words actually describing:

plop   splash   clang   trickle   snap

e.g. are they wet or dry sounds? What might make the sound? Use the words in sentences to show you know what they mean.

Handy hints for spelling

◆ Is the word spelt as it sounds? Does it contain any phonemes you already know?

◆ Does the word look right? Do you know any other words like it?

◆ Can you break the word into smaller parts? Which is the most difficult part of the word?

◆ Do you know what the word means?

◆ Have you used a word book or dictionary to help you?

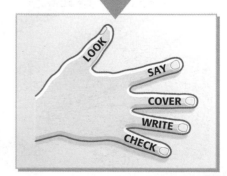

LOOK   SAY   COVER   WRITE   CHECK

Mr Fox

Lady Mary was young, and Lady Mary was fair. She had two brothers, and more lovers than she could count. But of them all, the bravest and most gallant was a Mr Fox, whom she met when she was down at her father's country house. No one knew who Mr Fox was; but he was certainly brave, and surely rich, and of all her lovers, Lady Mary cared for him alone. At last it was agreed upon between them that they should be married. Lady Mary asked Mr Fox where they should live, and he described to her his castle, and where it was, but, strange to say, did not ask her, or her brothers, to come and see it.

So one day, near the wedding-day, when her brothers were out, and Mr Fox was away for a day or two on business, as he said, Lady Mary set out for Mr Fox's castle. And after many searchings, she came at last to it, and a fine strong house it was, with high walls and a deep moat. And when she came up to the gateway, she saw written on it:

BE BOLD, BE BOLD

But as the gate was open, she went through it, and found no one there. So she went up to the doorway, and over it she found written:

BE BOLD, BE BOLD, BUT NOT TOO BOLD

Still she went on, till she came to the hall, and went up the broad stairs till she came to a door in the gallery, over which was written:

BE BOLD, BE BOLD, BUT NOT TOO BOLD,

LEST THAT YOUR HEART'S BLOOD SHOULD RUN COLD

But Lady Mary was a brave one, she was, and she opened the door, and what do you think she saw?

A British folk tale collected by Katherine M. Briggs

TEXT

1 Where did Lady Mary meet Mr Fox? What two things was she sure of about him?

2 Why was Mr Fox not at his castle?

3 Explain how the three messages change as Lady Mary walks through the castle.

4 Find three examples of words or phrases, e.g. 'once upon a time', that would only be written down in a folk tale like this.

5 Look at these six features of the story called *Mr Fox* and give some examples from other fairy stories or folk tales.

- **animals and humans marry, e.g.** *Beauty and the Beast* ● **live in a castle**
- **mysterious hero** ● **hero is not what he seems** ● **brave heroine** ● **strange messages**

6 Write what you think happens next in the story.

SENTENCE

1 Find three pronouns in the first paragraph of the passage.
Write next to them the nouns that they replace, e.g. she = Lady Mary.

2 Rewrite the sentences below to avoid repeating the nouns. Choose from these pronouns: I, she, mine, its, it, who, which, whom, ours. You will have to change the sentences.

a) The trainers in the shop were expensive. The trainers belonging to me were cheaper.
b) One door is green. The door leads to the playground.
c) He liked the CD. The CD had a bright cover.

3 Say what is wrong with this sentence. Rewrite it to make proper sense.

Be careful with dangerous pills in your bathroom. If children are about, lock them in a cupboard.

WORD

1 Write these words in a list, one beneath the other: guitar, circle, general, cat, pencil, rice, great, gym, gold, cell, tongue, Cyprus. Underline the 'c' or 'g' sound.
Write by the side of the word whether they are hard or soft sounds.

2 Read the first paragraph of the passage. Find and write down examples of soft and hard 'c' and 'g' words, e.g. could – hard 'c'.

3 *a)* Go back to your examples and circle the letter that comes after the 'c' or 'g'.
Decide if it is a vowel or a consonant. *b)* Write some rules to explain why some 'c' and 'g' sounds are hard or soft. *c)* Write some more soft 'c' and 'g' words.

The Ramayana

Our story begins in a magical kingdom in the Himalayas. Rama was a wonderful prince. When he met the beautiful Sita, he won her love by impressing her with his skill with his bow and arrows. But Rama's stepmother was jealous. She demanded of the king that he send Rama, Sita and his other devoted son, Laksmana into exile. The king loved his wife and his children, but because of his wife's trickery, he had made a foolish promise years before to do whatever she asked.

Cheated of their throne and banished, they lived happily in the deep Indian forest for fourteen years. Wandering through this forest, a young woman caught sight of Rama and instantly fell in love with him. He explained that he wanted nothing to do with her. Little did he know the trouble he was about to cause, because after some time, she returned to her own kingdom of Lanka – now Sri Lanka – to complain to her evil brother, Rawana, the King of the Demons.

To help his sister, Rawana sent a servant to Rama's forest, magically transformed into a deer. Rama loved hunting with his bow and arrows and chased the deer far into the dense forest. While he was away, Rawana kidnapped the defenceless Sita and flew with her through the air, back to his island.

Rama returned from his chase empty handed and was devastated to find his wife gone. Where was she? He knew who would help him. He called upon Hanuman, King of the Monkeys. His troops all over India would find the missing Sita. And he was right ... she was finally tracked down.

The monkey armies swarmed towards the island, itching for a fight. But how were they to cross the sea? All the monkeys clasped each other's tails and created a bridge for the rest of the invading army to charge over. This is just one of the miraculous tales told about the twelve-year war that they fought.

In the end, Rama killed Rawana with a magic arrow and became King of Lanka. Rama and Sita returned home to their mountain kingdom and their way was marked with lights of all kinds. Ever since then, the date has been marked by the festival of Diwali. At this time, fireworks are set off and there are lights everywhere. It is not just a festival of joy, but is a celebration of good winning against evil, of light triumphing over darkness.

A traditional Indian legend

TEXT

1 *a)* Where did Rama and Sita come from?
   b) How did Rama win the love of Sita?

2 *a)* Why were they sent into exile?   *b)* Who went with them?
   c) How long did their exile last?

3 Explain how Sita was kidnapped and how and where she was taken.

4 How did the monkeys help Rama to get Sita back?

5 How is the story of Rama and Sita now used in a religious way?

6 Here are seven features of *The Ramayana*. Find examples of the same features in
   Western stories, e.g. *The Ramayana* has a wicked stepmother, so does *Snow White*.

   - **heroic deeds**
   - **hero is sent into exile**
   - **heroine is kidnapped**
   - **fantastic creatures**
   - **magic is used**
   - **a battle between good and evil**

SENTENCE

1 Write a short version of these words, e.g. Road – Rd.
   street   telephone   approximately   number   United States of America

2 Look in a dictionary. Write out what these abbreviations mean: p.m., IOU, min, e.g., i.e.

3 Write down the most important fact in each of these sentences:
   a) This cake is made from many ingredients: eggs, flour, sugar, milk, nuts and honey.
   b) Fred has three good friends and they are Clive, Raj and James.

4 Write out these sentences in a shorter way, avoiding any repeated ideas:
   a) I was told to return back to school. *b)* These are the true facts.
   c) We crashed when the car reversed back into us. *d)* The lizard was of a very large size.

WORD

1 Write the opposites of these words: **open   black   small   down   energetic.**

2 Make opposites of these words using negative prefixes, e.g. 'in', 'mis', 'un', 'im'.
   colour   honest   behave   justice   polite   possible   welcome

3 Copy the chart. Underline the word meaning the opposite of the word on the left.

bright	new, dull, shiny, smart
demolish	old, reinforce, build, destroy
dangerous	holding, safe, ridiculous, silent

The Cataract at Lodore

This is part of a longer poem.

The cataract strong then plunges along;
Striking and raging as if a war waging
Its caverns and rocks among;
Rising and leaping, sinking and creeping,
Swelling and sweeping, showering and springing,
Plying and flinging, writhing and wringing,
Eddying and whisking, spouting and frisking,
Turning and twisting, around and around
With endless rebound ...

And threading and spreading and whizzing and hissing
And dripping and skipping and hitting and splitting,
And shining and twining and rattling and battling,
And shaking and quaking, and pouring and roaring,
And moaning and groaning;
And glittering and frittering, and gathering and feathering,
And whitening and brightening, and quivering and shivering,
And flurrying and scurrying, and thundering and floundering ...

Recoiling, turmoiling and toiling and boiling,
And flapping and rapping and clapping and slapping,
And curling and whirling and purling and twirling,
And thumping and bumping and jumping,
And dashing and flashing and splashing and clashing.

Robert Southey

TEXT

1 Is this a description of a slow or a fast stream? Write down three words from the poem which support your answer.

2 Do you think this stream is in a mountainous or a flat area? Say why.

3 What do you notice most about the words that the poet has used? Why do you think he chose this pattern of words? Give reasons.

4 Read the extract again. Where is the first full stop? What effect does this long sentence have? Does this help you to imagine the kind of stream this is? Say how.

5 Choose five of your favourite words from the poem. Look up any strange words in a dictionary. Say which of your five senses the words appeal to and explain why you chose them, e.g. moaning and groaning are mysterious sound words. They make me hear the strange noises the water makes as it bubbles among the rocks.

SENTENCE

1 Join each pair of sentences to make one sentence, using one of the conjunctions in the brackets.

a) I bought an ice cream for him. He did not buy one for me. (and/but)

b) Mum gets bad headaches. She watches too much TV. (but/because)

c) Dad has been ill for a year. He never complains. (also/although)

2 Rewrite the sentences below to make them more interesting, e.g. "Tracey ate her tea. She went out to play" is dull. This could be rewritten as: Having eaten her tea, Tracey went out to play.

a) Jim bought a car. He wanted to drive it every day.

b) Anne cut the cake. She gave it to her children.

c) Fred gave up smoking. He put on twelve pounds.

d) Eric broke his leg. He could not play football.

3 Circle the verbs in your new sentences. Explain what has happened to them.

WORD

1 Find the verbs ending in 'ing' in the first nine lines of the poem. Write the root verb like this: striking – strike

2 Circle the 'ing' in each verb in your chart. Look at the letter before it. Say what you notice about what happens when you add 'ing' to verbs ending in 'e'.

3 Now make a chart with verbs in line 11 of the poem, circling the 'ing' part and looking at the letters that come before. Say what differences you notice about how spelling changes when you add 'ing'.

4 *a)* Write a spelling rule about doubling the final consonant when you add 'ing' to words of one syllable. *b)* Find some other examples from the poem to prove the rule.

The Tomb of Tutankhamun

The tomb of Tutankhamun comprises four chambers, and is the smallest royal tomb in the Valley of the Kings, occupying only 83.6 square metres (900 square feet) of floor space. It had been hastily cut and never finished, with all but one room, the burial chamber, unlevelled and undecorated. Yet within it lay the greatest treasure ever found by any archaeologist.

The antechamber, 8 metres x 3.7 metres (26 feet x 12 feet) was dominated by three gilded wooden beds with carved animal heads. In front and on top of them were crammed chairs, stools and assorted boxes, mixed with bows and arrows, throwing-sticks and walking sticks, and flowers that seemed freshly picked. One of the walking sticks, a simple reed with an inscribed gold ferrule and knob, recorded that it had been cut by the little king's own hand. Under one of the beds, a long decorated box contained a trumpet, one of two discovered in

the tomb. (In 1939, it was sounded once again, fittingly in the Cairo Museum.)

To the left of the entrance lay a confused pile that proved to be two golden chariots, while to the right, two black and gold life-size statues enshrouded in tattered linen stood sentry against a plastered wall.

Under one of the beds, a low doorway could be seen. "Cautiously we crept under the couch, inserted our torch, and there before us lay another chamber, smaller than the first, but even more crowded with objects. The state of this room (afterwards called the annexe) simply defies description," Carter wrote. "Not a single square inch of floor remains vacant." Among the objects he found were low beds, used by the king in life, more chairs, and several superb gaming boards, inlaid in ivory and gold.

From Exploring the World of the Pharoahs *by Christine Hobson*

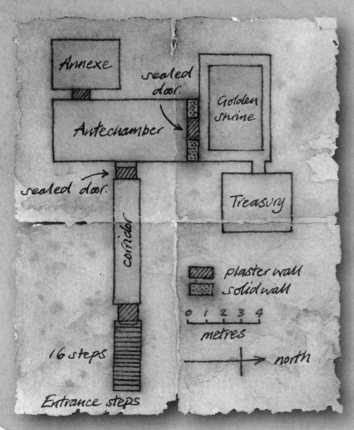

TEXT

1   How many rooms are there in Tutankhamun's tomb?

2   Which words in the first paragraph tell you that it had been made in a hurry and was not completed?

3   *a)* What took up most space in the antechamber?
    b) What do you find surprising about what else was in the room? Give reasons.

4   *a)* How did Carter find the final room? *b)* Say why he said "It defies description".

5   Here are eight features of the type of writing which aims to explain something. Find examples of each feature in the passage,
    e.g. Uses passive tense for verbs – 'was dominated by':

    ● **describes a step at a time**   ● **uses words to lead you through the explanation**
    ● **uses technical words**   ● **uses statistics**   ● **lists lots of detail**
    ● **quotes other people's views**   ● **uses diagrams to help**

SENTENCE

1   The word 'mummy' can have two meanings. Use it in two sentences to show the different meanings.

2   Use a dictionary to prove that each of these words can have two meanings. Write sentences to show the differences between them.

    mint   strike   coach   stick   plot

3   Explain why these sentences are ambiguous (have two meanings).
    Write them out so that they have one meaning.

    a) She found a van full of cows that had broken down.

    b) A newspaper headline read: AIRCRASH KILLS FATHER OF TEN.

    c) The team were shooting hard. At last Fred tried a shot with his head.
        It came off first time.

WORD

1   Write down 'cow' and 'bow' and say them. What do you notice about the spelling and the sounds of the words?

2   Write sentences to show two completely different meanings for these words: row, read, wind. Use a dictionary to help.

3   Sort out these 'ough' words into rhyming groups, e.g. ought, bought:
    enough   dough   tough   although   brought   plough   bought   drought

4   After looking carefully at your examples, write a definition of a homograph.

Bats

WILDLIFE FACTS

Bats manage to live alongside humans throughout Britain – you may even find them sharing your house. Don't worry though, these much misunderstood animals are not the evil creatures we often imagine them to be, but are simply flying mammals with a taste for insects.

British bats

In Britain there are fourteen species of bat, all of which are found on the south coast of England, with only seven or eight in the middle of England and decreasing to two or three in the north of Scotland. This variation is due to the greater availability of insects to feed on in the south, with its warmer climate and different farming methods; and possibly a greater number of roost sites. All the bats in this country are relatively small: the pipistrelle being one of the smallest, is just 5cm long, with a wing span of 20cm and weighing 4 grams (the same as a ten pence piece). One of the largest and most widespread is the noctule, reaching 8cm long and often mistaken for a swift as it flies so high soon after sunset.

Threats to bats

Numbers of bats have been declining over the years due to loss of roost sites, timber treatment of roofs using chemicals toxic to bats, pesticides killing their prey and a dramatic loss of appropriate feeding sites. For these reasons bats are protected by the law under the Wildlife & Countryside Act 1981. It is illegal to harm bats or disturb their roost sites. If you find a sick or injured bat, or think that you have a roost in your house, then contact English Nature (01733 340345) who will put you in touch with a licensed bat worker.

Bat myths

The saying 'as blind as a bat' is entirely wrong, bats can see perfectly well although not in colour. Bats do not get tangled in long hair when flying, as they have excellent 'night vision' using echo-location – emitting a high frequency sound which usually can't be heard by people. The bat listens for the returning echo of the sound from nearby objects and can build up a clear picture of its surroundings. The classic image of a bat drinking blood is linked to the Dracula myth. However, out of almost 1,000 species of bat around the world only three lap up blood from large animals and the comforting news is that they all live in South or Central America.

Bat friends

Bats are under threat – so consider making your house and garden more bat-friendly:

- put up bat boxes or install a bat brick for easy access to your roof space;
- encourage bats' food (night flying insects) by planting night scented flowers such as honeysuckle or evening primrose;
- tell English Nature if you think bats are roosting in your house;
- take advice from English Nature before treating your home with chemicals or using sprays in the garden.

TEXT

1 *a)* How many types of bat are there in Britain? *b)* Where are they mostly found?
c) Why are most found there?

2 *a)* Give three reasons why numbers of bats have been declining over the years.
b) What has the government done to help them?

3 What two things is it now illegal to do to bats?

4 Write down three things that you could do to help bats survive and say why they would be useful.

5 The passage is divided into sections using subheadings.
In which section would you find the following:

a) ideas linked to the Dracula story
b) how to make your garden more bat-friendly
c) information about the Wildlife and Countryside Act
d) the effect of the climate in southern England on bats
e) the sizes of bats in the United Kingdom.

SENTENCE

Choose the correct words to complete these sentences:

a) I (seen, saw) her when she (came, come) to school.
b) Ranjit (did, done) his homework very well.
c) In the shop they helped (theirselves, themselves) to some sweets (which, what) were on the shelf.
d) We (was, were) hungry but we didn't have (no, any) food.
e) Who (did, done) (them, those) wonderful paintings on the wall?
f) She could (of, have) (took, taken) a smaller piece of cake!
g) There (are, is) three layers in a trifle.

WORD

1 Find opposites for:
cheap   easy   artificial   rich   brilliant
Use a thesaurus to help you.

2 List these words for 'hot' in order, from the hottest to the least hot.
Use a dictionary and check the meanings carefully.
muggy   scalding   boiling   tepid   fiery   blistering   luke-warm   scorching

3 Use the words in question 2 in sentences to show the differences between them.

Using poems as frameworks

1 Read the poem in Unit 2.8 again. Write your own version of the first nine lines, using the pattern of the poem. Make use of the new words in the Word box. Use a thesaurus and add some more of your own. You could start:

The river is strong and gurgles along

Oozing and gushing …

Word box

gurgle	rush	gush
meander	ripple	ooze
waterfall	tinkle	rush
whirlpool	torrent	fountain
swirl	jet	bubble
spurt	cataract	splash
surge	swell	

◆ Have fun with the sounds of the words.

◆ What kinds of words will achieve your effect – hard sounds or soft sounds (see Unit 2.6)?

◆ What words can you find that make use of onomatopoeia? (see Unit 2.4)?

◆ Will you use the words as nouns or verbs, e.g. a gurgle or the river gurgles?

◆ Which tense will you use for the verbs, e.g. will you use the same 'ing' tense like the poet, e.g. gurgling, or will you use the past tense, e.g. the river gurgled?

2 Use a similar pattern to write your own piece to describe a stormy sea or a thunderstorm. Make your own Word box.

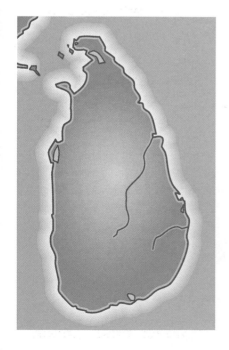

Using myths and fairy tales for other kinds of writing

3 Read Unit 2.7 again. Imagine you are working for the Tourist Board of Sri Lanka and you are given the job of using the story of the Ramayana to encourage tourists to come to the island. Write a brochure advertising Sri Lanka as an island of myths and legends. You could start: Come to the magical island of Sri Lanka, where myths come to life … You can visit the place where …

Remember:

◆ You will not just be writing the story, you will be trying to persuade your readers.

◆ What parts of the story will be attractive to people wanting to visit the Far East?

◆ You could design and make your brochure and find or draw maps and pictures.

Finding information and communicating it

A good way to make notes from a passage is to use a chart or a table. You need to:

◆ decide from the start what information you need to find. This could be written as your title.

◆ write the details of what you need in the columns of your charts as key words or key questions.

◆ write in your own words and do not copy out parts of the passage.

4 Read Units 2.9 and 2.10 again. Copy and complete these two charts.

Myths about bats

myth	truth
blind as a bat	can see – but shortsighted

What Carter found in Tutankhamun's tomb

room	what was in it
antechamber	gold beds …

5 Explain what myths there are about bats and why they are not correct. Write a short passage of description – two or three paragraphs – from your chart. Do not look again at the passage.

6 Imagine you are a radio reporter with Carter when he discovers Tutankhamun's tomb. Write your script for broadcasting. Remember:

◆ this is not just an account of the facts, it is one person talking to his listeners

◆ think about the style, e.g. tenses, used for radio broadcasts

◆ how will you make the scene real for listeners as they have no pictures? You will have to describe the scene in detail

◆ you will need to follow Carter through the tomb, room by room to build up a sense of excitement

◆ you will need to interview Carter to see how he feels.

Editing checklist

Form of writing
Have you done what you set out to do?
Have you used the right style?
Have you chosen a good title?
Have you presented your work properly?

Check your sentences
Do they make sense?
Do you need to make any more interesting?

Check your punctuation
Capital letters and full stops?
Speech marks?
Are commas used correctly?

Handwriting or word processing
Which will make it easier to read and present your ideas?

Check your spelling
Use dictionaries and a thesaurus to check words you are not sure about.

Do you need illustrations?
What will be the most appropriate?
Where will they fit in the design?

Produce final version

> How are you getting on with things in the chart? If you need extra practice try the activities shown.

Grammar and punctuation	Nouns and pronouns	1
	Making sentences shorter – summarising	2
	Constructing sentences	3
	Agreement with verbs	4
Spelling, phonics and vocabulary	Consonants – soft and hard c and g sounds	5
	Consonants – doubling the final consonant	6
	Homographs	7
	Antonyms	8
	Ambiguity	9

1 Copy and complete the sentences using pronouns.

a) When Tracy and … stopped talking, the teacher told … to take out our stories but not to write any more of ….

b) The teacher was angry and told the class that if … did not be quiet and finish the work, … would have to finish … at breaktime.

c) I forgot to talk to Ashok last week so I spoke to … yesterday when I finally saw …

d) After school I found him. "I'm fed up of … telling stories about …," I shouted.

2 *a)* Write shorter versions of: two o'clock in the afternoon, five o'clock in the morning, please reply as soon as possible, happening very often.

b) Use a dictionary to write one word that means the same as: to rub out,   to leave your own country to go and live in another country,   a false statement which aims to deceive,   wanting something to drink.

3 Tracey cleaned her mum's car. They drove to the park, is not very interesting. It could read: When Tracey had cleaned her mum's car, they drove to the park. Join these sentences in a similar way:

a) Jim wrote a letter. He posted it. *b)* Bev learned how to drive. She was never at home. *c)* Glen made the coffee. She sat down to read her book.
Go back over your answers and explain how the verbs have changed.

4 Choose the correct word and write out the sentences:

a) There wasn't (no, any) milk.

b) I should not have (give, given) the book to (she, her).

c) They were so hungry that after they had (ate, eaten) the cake and (drank, drunk) their coffee, they helped (themselves, theirselves) to more.

5 Write these words:

guitar except electric France pencil Cyprus general coal city tongue generate concert great disguise

Underline the 'c' and 'g' sounds. Say if they are soft or hard.

6 Add 'ing', 'er' and 'ed' to these words if it is possible:

skip hot swim dig fail cool rob

Check your spelling in a dictionary.

7 *a)* Sort these 'ow' words into two columns according to their sound:

now show low owl towel snow growl grown

b) Put these four words into the columns:

row sow row sew

What do you notice?

c) Write sentences to show two different meanings of these four words.

8 *a)* Write the opposites of: black hit early go fast huge

b) List these words for *cold* in order – start with the coldest and go to the least cold.

Use a dictionary to check meanings carefully.

glacial chilly freezing frosty wintry

9 *a)* Write sentences to show two different meanings for:

score bulb light

b) Explain why this advertisement is ambiguous (has two meanings). Write it out so that it has one meaning.

> ## *Still getting headaches?*
> ### Allow us to test your eyes to help you remove them.

Handy hints for spelling

◆ Is the word spelt as it sounds? Does it contain any phonemes you already know?

◆ Does the word look right? Do you know any other words like it?

◆ Can you break the word into smaller parts? Which is the most difficult part of the word?

◆ Do you know what the word means?

◆ Have you used a word book or dictionary to help you?

LOOK SAY COVER WRITE CHECK

Secrets

In this story from India, Rohan is told off by his teacher. He is on his way home, with a letter for his parents.

But once he reached the big grey banyan tree that was the only tree in the lane, and found that the cobbler who usually sat under it, mending broken old shoes, was not there, he sat down in its shade, hiding himself in the folds of the great trunk, and sobbed a little with anger. He had not been able to get his sums right although he had tried. He had dropped the ink bottle by accident and not to spoil the teacher's white shoes. Perhaps it was bad of him to pull a face but how could he help it when things were going so badly? Now he was afraid to go home and hand the letter to his father, who would be very angry and beat him. He sometimes did, and often scolded him.

So Rohan hid there in the folds of the grey tree-trunk, and poked with a stick at the seeds dropped on the ground by the parrots that ate the red berries of the tree. He was so angry and afraid that he poked and poked with the stick till he had dug quite a deep hole in the dust. In that hole he found a little grey lump of rubber – a plain piece of rubber that some other schoolboy might have dropped there long ago. He picked it up and rolled it about between his fingers.

"I wish it were a magic rubber," he said, sobbing a little. "I would rub out the whole school, like this – like this – " and he stepped out to look down the lane at the boys' school that stood at the end of it, and angrily rubbed at the air with the grey lump of rubber.

Then he stopped, his hand still in mid-air, his mouth still open, and his hair began to stand up on his head as it did on his neighbour's cat's back when she saw his dog.

Something very, very strange had happened. The school had vanished. He had really rubbed it out! The tall, three-storeyed house on its left, with its latticed balconies and green roof, was still there, and on the other side the tin-roofed warehouse where timber was stacked stood there too, but in between them, where the school had been, there was now a patch of earth.

Anita Desai

TEXT

1 Where did Rohan stop on his way home? Why was he able to sit in this place today?

2 Give three reasons why he was angry at his punishment.

3 Why did Rohan not want to go home with the letter? What might happen?

4 What two reactions show us Rohan was shocked and surprised by what the rubber had done?

5 Copy down the statements that are true about the buildings around the school:
   a) The house was on its right.
   b) The house had three floors.
   c) Its roof was made of metal.
   d) It had balconies with open sides.
   e) People worked in the building to the right.

6 Read the passage again. Write down details from the story that show the story is not set in Britain, e.g. trees, animals, buildings, people's attitudes, any words you do not recognise.

SENTENCE

1 Copy these sentences and put commas where they are needed:
   a) The rugby team formed up jumped about a bit huddled together for a team talk and started the game.
   b) In the jungle the trees were tall rounded knotty brown and dreary. Their branches were long thin weedy looking and hanging with moss.
   c) As he looked up he was aware of the blue sky the clouds the bright sun the leaves and their shadows.

2 Write out these sentences, putting in commas correctly:
   a) When we finally reached the coast we saw the blue sea sparkling in front of us.
   b) Do you want to go too?
   c) Fred as usual wanted to play the game first.
   d) Of course he stayed on the computer for hours.

WORD

1 Write down the five vowels. Copy these words and put in the correct vowels:
   t _ rr _ f _ c   _ nt _ r _ st   s _ p _ r _ t _   d _ ff _ r _ nt   b _ _ _ t _ f _ l

2 In the words in question 1, circle the vowels you think often get missed because they are not heard.

3 Write out these words and put in the correct vowels:
   _ xtr _ _ rd _ n _ ry   c _ mp _ ny   d _ scr _ pt _ _ n   c _ rp _ t   fr _ _ d _ m

4 Write them out again, breaking them into syllables, e.g. *se-par-ate.*
   Circle the vowels which you think often get missed out because they are not heard.

5 Use the *Look, say, cover, write, check* method to learn these words.

The Little House in the Big Woods

Laura and her family were some of the first people to move into the 'wild west' of the USA in the 1870s. Here she learns of danger.

Laura and Mary had never seen a town. They had never seen a store. They had never seen even two houses standing together. But they knew that in a town there were many houses, and a store full of candy and calico and other wonderful things – powder, and shot, and salt, and store sugar.

They knew that Pa would trade his furs to the storekeeper for beautiful things from town, and all day they were expecting the presents he would bring them. When the sun sank low above the treetops and no more drops fell from the tips of the icicles they began to watch eagerly for Pa.

The sun sank out of sight, the woods grew dark, and he did not come. Ma started supper and set the table, but he did not come. It was time to do the chores, and still he had not come.

Ma said that Laura might come with her while she milked the cow. Laura could carry the lantern.

So Laura put on her coat and Ma buttoned it up. And Laura put her hands into her red mittens that hung by a red yarn string around her neck, while Ma lighted the candle in the lantern.

Laura was proud to be helping Ma with the milking, and she carried the lantern very carefully. Its sides were of tin, with places cut in them for the candle-light to shine through.

When Laura walked behind Ma on the path to the barn, the little bits of candle-light from the lantern leaped all around her on the snow. The night was not yet quite dark. The woods were dark, but there was a grey light on the snowy path, and in the sky there were a few faint stars. The stars did not look as warm and bright as the little lights that came from the lantern.

Laura was surprised to see the dark shape of Sukey, the brown cow, standing at the barnyard gate. Ma was surprised too.

It was too early in the spring for Sukey to be let out in the Big Woods to eat grass. She lived in the barn. But sometimes on warm days Pa left the door of her stall open so she could come into the barnyard. Now Ma and Laura saw her behind the bars, waiting for them.

Ma went up to the gate, and pushed against it to open it. But it did not open very far, because there was Sukey, standing against it. Ma said:

"Sukey, get over!" She reached across the gate and slapped Sukey's shoulder.

Just then one of the dancing bits of light from the lantern jumped between the bars of the gate, and Laura saw long, shaggy, black fur, and two little, glittering eyes. Sukey had thin, short, brown fur. Sukey had large, gentle eyes.

Ma said, "Laura, walk back to the house."

So Laura turned around and began to walk towards the house. Ma came behind her. When they had gone part way, Ma snatched her up, lantern and all, and ran. Ma ran with her into the house, and slammed the door.

Then Laura said, "Ma, was it a bear?"

Laura Ingalls Wilder

TEXT

1 Where had Laura's father gone? What was he aiming to do there?

2 What season of the year was Pa away? Give your reasons. When was he due to return?

3 Give three examples to show that Laura and her sister lived their life away from other people.

4 Why was Laura surprised when she got to the barnyard? Give reasons for this. Why was what they found in the barnyard so dangerous?

5 Find information from the passage about the story setting. Look for details of:
   ●the countryside ●the season ●the time of day ●the farm ●the time in history

SENTENCE

1 Write out these shortened words and then write them in full, e.g. he's – he is.
   he's I'll you've we're it's they'll

2 Put the shortened versions into sentences to show you understand them.

3 Write out the short form of these words, putting in apostrophes:
she will	**he will**	**is not**	**was not**	**were not**
it has	**I would**	**I had**	**I have**	

4 Write out the short form of these words, putting in apostrophes: shall not, will not, cannot. What do you notice is unusual about the number of missing letters?

5 In speech, we use apostrophes to show letters missed out, e.g. "I 'ate 'im," he shouted. Use shortened forms of these words in sentences.
   hungry telephone him them house hang

WORD

1 Write out these words, putting in the missing vowels, e.g. b – te = bite.
   car _   cle _ n   shar _   h _ r   rid _   b _ y   skat _   w _ it

2 Add 'ing' and 'ed' to the words in question 1, if possible.
   Check your spelling in a dictionary. When the word ends in an 'e', what happens?

3 Now add 'ing' and 'ed' to these other single-syllable words. Check your spelling.
   fire cure move prove change

4 Add 'ing' and 'ed' to these longer words. Does the same thing happen?
   manage rescue complete surface persuade believe

Redwings Horse Sanctuary

REDWINGS HORSE SANCTUARY

Redwings Horse Sanctuary was founded in 1984 to provide a caring home for horses, ponies, donkeys and mules. These animals have been rescued from neglect and the threat of being killed. Our work is about reducing the suffering of equines. Every week we take in animals which really need our care and attention. We aim to give them a home until the end of their days. At present we care for over 1,000 animals and, because more and more help is needed, sadly we expect that our workload will continue to grow.

With the help of our caring staff and volunteers, Redwings looks after its animals, makes new arrivals happy and comfortable and raises money to keep them. Our horses live as natural a life as possible. During the winter they run free in well-maintained paddocks. In summer extra land is leased for them to graze in.

It is very sad to see the animals who have suffered. It is also rewarding to watch them get better and make friends in the Sanctuary. They come to Redwings for many reasons: some have been neglected or were going to be killed. Some are injured or are unwanted by their owners. The main reason for the large number of unwanted equines is that people are not sensible when breeding them.

Redwings spends a lot of time and money on education. We warn people about the problems of overbreeding the animals. We think this happens not because of neglect, but because owners do not think about the results of their actions. Our trained Welfare Officers help and give advice to owners on the care and feeding of horses and donkeys. We give out free information sheets about how to care for their animals to anyone who asks. We also produce leaflets, such as this one, and send out a regular newsletter which gives our views and describes the work we do.

Hill Top Farm, Hall Lane, Frettenham, Norwich NR12 7RW
Tel: 01603 737432   Registered Charity No: 295763

TEXT

1 What do you think an 'equine' is? Look in a dictionary.

2 How many horses are cared for at the sanctuary?

3 Why are the writers of this leaflet 'sad' that they will have to have more animals in their sanctuary?

4 What are four main reasons why animals come to the sanctuary?

5 Why is education such an important part of their programme?
What do their Welfare Officers do?

6 Which of these statements do you think is true? Give your reasons.

   a) This leaflet gives you information as well as persuading you to support the charity.
   b) It uses pictures so you will feel sorry for attractive animals.
   c) It uses persuasive language, e.g. 'desperately', 'slaughter', 'enormous task', to make you support them and send money.

SENTENCE

1 Write out the correct parts of the verb 'to be'.

Today: I am, you ..., he/she/it ..., we ..., you ..., they are

Yesterday: I was, you ..., he/she/it ..., we ..., you ..., they were

2 Write out these sentences, using the correct form of the verb and of the other words in brackets.

   a) The girls (was/were) asleep in (there/their) caravan when the fire (starting/started/starts).
   b) He (have/has) had to fight to help (him/he/it) keep his dog.
   c) I am certain that the girls (will/shall) swim (well/good) tomorrow.

WORD

1 Copy and complete this chart with ten more words that have a sound like the 'ee' phoneme. Use a dictionary to help you.

ee	ea	ie	ei	e

2 Write out the following words putting in 'ie' or 'ei'. Use your dictionary to check.

ch _ _ f   rel _ _ ve   dec _ _ ve   n _ _ ce   f _ _ ld   bel _ _ ve   n _ _ ghbour

3 Put the words in question 2 into three groups:

   ● **'ee' sound made by 'ie'**   ● **'ee' sound made by 'ei'**   ● **not an 'ee' sound**

4 Write a rule to help you spell words with 'ie' or 'ei'. Find five exceptions to the rule.

Night Mail

This poem was written to be the 'voice-over' for a film. It is about the train which takes the mail from London to Scotland overnight. This part of the poem describes the train arriving in Scotland. When you have worked on the excerpt from the poem, you should try reading it aloud to really enjoy it.

Past cotton grass and moorland boulder
Shovelling white steam over her shoulder.
Snorting noisily as she passes
Silent miles of wind-bent grasses.

Birds turn their heads as she approaches,
Stare from the bushes at her black-faced coaches.
Sheep-dogs cannot turn her course,
They slumber on with paws across.
In the farm she passes no one wakes,
But a jug in the bedroom gently shakes.

Dawn freshens, the climb is done.
Down towards Glasgow she descends
Towards the steam tugs yelping in a glade of cranes,
Set on the dark plain like gigantic chessmen.
All Scotland waits for her:
In the dark glens, beside the pale-green lochs
Men long for news.

Letters of thanks, letters from banks,
Letters of joy from girl and boy,
Receipted bills and invitations
To inspect new stock or visit relations,
And applications for situations
And timid lovers' declarations
And gossip, gossip from all the nations.

W. H. Auden

TEXT

1 *a)* What words in the first verse show the poet is describing a steam train?
b) How does he imagine the steam moving?
c) What noise does he describe?

2 Explain how the two animals mentioned react to the train passing.

3 In verse 3, the poet imagines the scene below him in the countryside to be like a chessboard. *a)* What could the squares on the chessboard be? *b)* What does he say reminds him of chess pieces?

4 Why is 'all Scotland waiting' for the train? Give your reasons.

5 Write down five types of letter that the train is carrying.

6 *a)* Find and write down two sets of couplets from the poem. *b)* How does the poem rhyme differently in the last part of the poem?

SENTENCE

1 Put these examples into two columns; *whole sentences* and *phrases*.

- **The frost was sharp** - **the full moon** - **letters and mounds of parcels**
- **From house to house, he moved slowly** - **on the clean mat in the hallway**

2 In the chart below, match up a phrase from column A to a phrase from column B. Join the two phrases with a verb and write the sentence you have made:

Column A	Column B
the van driver	behind the dark hill
young children	by the side of the road
a blazing sun	on the Christmas tree

3 Write sentences using each of these phrases:

- **into the lead** - **the three of us again** - **cats and dogs** - **absolutely clear**

WORD

1 Make these nouns plural: **baby lady chimney donkey family valley**

2 Sort your answers into two columns, under the headings 'just add s' and 'change the y to something else'. Write a rule about this. What do you notice?

3 Use these verbs ending in 'y' in sentences. Use present and past tenses, e.g. He cries when he wants his mum. I cried at the end of the sad film.

- **to cry** - **to deny** - **to fry** - **to spy** - **to destroy** - **to buy** - **to stay**

4 Write the verbs in a chart under the headings 'just add s' and 'change the y to something else'. Write a rule about this. What do you notice?

Letters about fox-hunting

1

Dear Sirs,

Firstly, foxes are killers. I talked to a shepherd last week who told me he had lost ten new-born lambs, all senselessly slaughtered by foxes. Don't tell me that it is cruel to hunt foxes. Surely, the general public knows that they are pests and need to be exterminated? Are we expected to put up with this for ever? This sport – and it is a sport – is a part of our culture in the countryside. I would ask these do-gooders to come to my farm and hear the sounds of chickens in the hen-house being attacked by a fox in the night. This is cruel. The fox doesn't even eat them very often!

Yours,

2

Dear Sir,

The writer of last week's letter needs to check his facts. If foxes are scavengers, then they keep down harmful animals for farmers. The fox is helping clear up the countryside. Leave them alone! If the farmer is worried about his hen-house, it wouldn't be difficult to make it more secure: 98% of poultry are quite safe from fox attack.

With all good wishes,

3

Dear Sir,

I am not in favour of fox-hunting but I can see that some way of keeping the fox population down is essential. They are known to be bigger carriers of rabies than dogs in this country. If the fox population becomes too big then food will be scarce and starvation will result. This is more cruel, surely, than hunting foxes for sport?

Yours faithfully,

4

Sir or Madam,

Fox-hunting is one of the cruellest 'sports' in this country and should be banned. Every right-thinking person must know that poor, defenceless animals are hunted down by whole packs of dogs so human beings can have fun. Do you know that when a hunter first kills a fox he or she is smeared with the animal's blood? There are alternative methods of keeping down populations but the traps used by farmers and poison are both cruel. Surely we are all civilized human beings around here?

Yours disgustedly,

TEXT

1 What does the writer say in letter 1 to show that foxes are killers?
Why is it surprising to this writer that the fox should attack his hens?

2 What argument does the writer of letter 2 use to show that foxes are useful animals to farmers? What is his solution to the problems of the writer of letter 1?

3 Why does the writer of letter 3 think foxes are a danger to people? Why else is he in favour of killing some of them?

4 Give one reason why the writer of letter 4 thinks hunting is cruel.

5 What other methods of killing foxes are given? Why are they not suitable?

6 Copy and complete this chart with information from all the letters.

For fox-hunting	Against fox-hunting
kill lambs	keep down pests

SENTENCE

1 Add a clause of your own to make these sentences more interesting. Use 'because' or 'if' as connectives, e.g. I do not like your hat because it is bright green.

a) He lost his job. *b)* Your teacher will get very angry. *c)* My car skidded off the road. *d)* She was never afraid. *e)* He will win the prize.

2 Write sentences and include these clauses in them:

a) because I hated it
b) if you press that button
c) so he stayed in bed
d) so that he could reach the books
e) when it stops raining
f) who scored a goal
g) whose coat was torn

WORD

1 Write the present and the past tenses of these verbs, like this: I am running – I was running.

to run   to read   to eat   to type   to laugh   to choose   to come

2 Now write the simple form of each past tense, e.g. he laughed. Circle the verbs you can just add 'ed' to. Underline the verbs where the root word changes.

3 'Froze' is the past tense of the verb 'to freeze'. Use the past tense of these verbs in sentences: choose, wear, write, eat, know – e.g. Yesterday, I chose.

Poems as models – writing couplets

Read *Night Mail* again in Unit 3.4.
Most of the poem is written in couplets
and the last words rhyme.

> *Past cotton grass and moorland* **boulder**
> *Shovelling white steam over her* **shoulder**.

Couplets have to follow a pattern.
These lines have four beats or stresses in them.
Try reading the lines. Tap out where the stresses are:

> **Shov**elling **white** steam **over** her **shoul**der.
> **Snor**ting **noisi**ly **as** she **pass**es.

1 Look carefully at the picture. Find a group
of children and write a couplet about them.
When you have written a few sets of couplets, write them
out as a complete poem called 'Children's Games'.
Here is an example using the poem's rhymes to help:

> Here comes a boy, huge as a boulder
> Laughing merrily over his shoulder.
> The blind boy rolls his barrel to the end
> Pushing and pushing, not hearing his friend.

Continuing a story – adding dialogue

2 Read Unit 3.1 again. Imagine you are Rohan. How would you describe what happened to your parents when you got home? Continue the story using dialogue (speech).

Remember:

- ◆ Words spoken by someone must be inside speech marks.
- ◆ Do not close speech marks without a piece of punctuation.
- ◆ Always start a new line when someone new begins to speak.

3 What do you think Laura, her sister and her mother said to each other when they locked themselves in their cabin? Read Unit 3.2 again and write more of their story by using speech. Follow the rules.

Using plans to write an argument

The words in this list all help you to persuade people when you write an argument.

Firstly   if   then   thus   therefore   so   but   however   furthermore   nevertheless   moreover   whereas

Write an argument by completing the sentences:

4 I believe that eating meat is wrong because …

Firstly …

Another reason would be that …

Moreover …

Therefore …

5 *It is not right that we have to go to bed early.*

I believe this because …

Another reason is …

because …

The result of this is …

But …

Nevertheless …

Therefore …

6 Now write arguments *against* these points of view. Use some of the other persuasion words in the list.

Proof-reading

Spelling

- ◆ Check the spelling. Use a dictionary.
- ◆ Make your own spelling list.
- ◆ Use a computer spell check.

Punctuation

- ◆ Have you written in sentences?
- ◆ Have you used capital letters at the beginning and full stops at the end?
- ◆ Have you used correct punctuation for speech?

Paragraphs

- ◆ Do you need to set your writing out in sections?
- ◆ Have you used paragraphs correctly?

How are you getting on with things in the chart? If you need extra practice try the activities shown.

Grammar and punctuation	Agreement between parts of sentences	1
	Phrases	2
	Clauses	3
	Commas	4
	Apostrophes – contractions	5
Spelling, phonics and vocabulary	Unstressed vowels in polysyllabic words	6
	Spelling patterns for vowels – omit e	7
	Spelling patterns for vowels – i before e	8
	Spelling patterns for vowels – y to ies	9
	Transforming words – changing tenses	10

1 Write out these sentences. Choose the correct word in the brackets:

a) We (was/were) not there. We didn't see (nobody/anybody).

b) It was (me/I) (what/who) (done/did) it.

c) The window had been (broke/broken) but we (was/were) not responsible.

d) We (have/had) heard the singer the day before.

2 *a)* Write complete sentences using these phrases:

over the bridge   at the foot of the stairs
on the surface of the moon   under the stars
in the middle of India

b) Finish these sentences putting in a phrase that tells us when:

Cuckoos build their nests … The skateboard was invented …
The moon disappears … Mankind first printed books …

3 *a)* Add a clause of your own to make these sentences more interesting. Use 'because' or 'if', e.g. I do not like your hat because it is bright green

a) She sat next to him   b) Pull out the plug
c) His jacket was never the same again

b) Add a sentence to these clauses:

a) because I never learned it   b) if you pull the handle
c) so he never visited   d) when I come home
e) so that he could play on the computer

4 Copy this passage. Put in ten commas where they are needed.

I bought my Christmas presents yesterday. I got three games two books one new pen but no boring pairs of socks. Ranjit who lives across the road gave me a new pencil, a pencil case, a ruler and some paper last year. Tracy my other best friend at school forgot to buy me anything at all!

5 Write out this passage. Put in apostrophes correctly.

Im going to the party at eight o clock. Ive hired a new costume so it wont be boring. Its easy to get there. Ill go on the bus. Theyve told me the address.

6 *a)* Write out these words. Put in the correct vowels:

extr _ _ rd _ n _ ry   d _ scr _ pt _ _ n   c _ rp _ t
fre _ d _ m   pois _ n _ us   port _ ble   int _ r _ st

b) Break the words into syllables.

e.g. | se | par | ate | has three syllables

Draw boxes around the syllables. Circle the vowels you think get missed out because they are not heard.

7 *a)* Add 'ing' and 'ed' to these words. Check your spelling.

score   hire   hear   fire   cure
bite   wear   ride   prove

b) Add 'ing' and 'ed' to these longer words:

create   argue   deny   manage   complete   surface

c) When the word ends in an 'e', what happens?

8 *a)* Write out the following words putting in 'ie' or 'ei'. Use your dictionary to check:

th _ _ f   ch _ _ f   w _ _ rd   rec _ _ pt
rel _ _ ve   h _ _ ght   p _ _ ce   sh _ _ ld
for _ _ gn   dec _ _ ve   gr _ _ ve

9 *a)* Use 'he' in front of these verbs, e.g. he tries:

to try to cry to fry to spy to buy to play

b) What do you notice about verbs that end in a vowel and 'y' and verbs that end in a consonant and 'y'?

10 Put these verbs in past and future tenses, e.g. I swim. I swam:

swim   begin   drink   throw   am

- Is the word spelt as it sounds? Does it contain any phonemes you already know?

- Does the word look right? Do you know any other words like it?

- Can you break the word into smaller parts? Which is the most difficult part of the word?

- Do you know what the word means?

- Have you used a word book or dictionary to help you?

LOOK SAY COVER WRITE CHECK

Hunter Poems of the Yoruba

The Yoruba are a group of people who live in West Africa. These poems were learnt by heart by the Yoruba people to describe the animals which they hunted. The poems were only recently translated and written down.

Leopard

Gentle hunter
his tail plays on the ground
while he crushes the skull.

Beautiful death
who puts on a spotted robe
when he goes to his victim.

Playful killer
whose loving embrace
splits the antelope's heart.

From the Yoruba, translated by Ulli Beier

Elephant

Elephant, a spirit in the bush,
Elephant who brings death.
He swallows a whole palmfruit
thorns and all.
He tramples down the grass
with his mortar legs.
Wherever he walks
the grass is forbidden to stand up again.
He tears a man like an old rag
and hangs him up in the tree.
With his single hand
he pulls two palm trees to the ground.
If he had two hands
he would tear the heaven to shreds.
An elephant is not a load for an old man –
nor for a young man either.

TEXT

1 Give two examples from the 'Elephant' poem to show how strong the elephant is.

2 What is the elephant's 'hand'? If the elephant had two of these, what does the poet say would be the result?

3 Write down the simile used in this poem about how the elephant kills.
What picture does this simile give you of the elephant? Give your reasons.

4 Read the first lines of the verses in *Leopard*. What impression of the animal is given by the use of the words 'gentle', 'beautiful' and 'playful'?

5 Now read the last lines. What different pictures do these lines give you?
Give reasons. Explain the differences.

6 Which of these statements do you think are true about the point of view of the poet? Give your reasons. *a)* The poet hates the animals. *b)* The poet respects but fears the animals. *c)* The poet thinks the animals are cruel.

SENTENCE

1 Copy these sentences. Underline the prepositions:
   a) Suddenly I noticed my path through the jungle was blocked by a huge, fallen tree.
   b) That clock in the corner behind the large door is over a hundred years old.
   c) My Dalmatian puppy lives in a kennel behind the house beside the garden shed.

2 Use these prepositions in sentences: under, over, across, before, between.

3 Change the meanings of the following sentences by changing the prepositions, e.g. He walked *over* the bridge. He walked *under* the bridge. He walked *beside* the bridge.
   a) Bev stepped over the huge puddle in the road. *b)* The policeman on a brown horse rode behind the carriage. *c)* My friends swam down the stream with the fast current.

WORD

1 The names of the days of our week come from the names of gods and goddesses. Which days of the week come from these names:
   Saturn   Woden   Moon   Frig   Thor   Tiw

2 Use your dictionary to find out which countries these sports started in:
   baseball   skiing   karate   polo   tobogganing

3 Find out which countries gave us these words:
   moccasin   bungalow   tomato   tycoon   boomerang   chocolate   banana   safari

4 Find out what these expressions mean and where they came from:
   per annum   au pair   de luxe   hors-d'oeuvres   anno domini

Carrie's War

Carrie and her brother Nick are evacuated from London to Wales during the Second World War. They arrive and nervously wait to be 'chosen' by a family.

Surely you can take two, Miss Evans?" "Two girls, perhaps. Not a boy and a girl, I'm afraid. I've only the one room, see, and my brother's particular."

Particular about what, Carrie wondered. But Miss Evans looked nice; a little like a red squirrel Carrie had once seen, peering round a tree in a park. Reddish brown hair and bright button eyes, and a shy, quivering look.

Carrie said, "Nick sleeps in my room at home because he has bad dreams sometimes. I always look after him and he's no trouble at all."

Miss Evans looked doubtful. "Well, I don't know what my brother will say. Perhaps I can chance it." She smiled at Carrie. "There's pretty eyes you have, girl! Like green glass!"

Carrie smiled back. People didn't often notice her when Nick was around. His eyes were dark blue, like their mother's. She said, "Oh, Nick's the pretty one, really."

Miss Evans walked fast. She was a little woman, not much taller than Carrie, but she seemed strong as a railway porter, carrying their cases as if they weighed nothing. Out of the hall, down the street. They stopped outside a grocery shop with the name Samuel Isaac Evans above the door and Miss Evans took a key from her bag. She said, "There's a back way and you'll use that, of course, but we'll go through the front for the once, as my brother's not here."

The shop was dim and smelled mustily pleasant. Candles and tarred kindling, and spices, Carrie thought wrinkling her nose. A door at the back led into a small room with a huge desk almost filling it. "My brother's office," Miss Evans said in a hushed voice and hurried them through into a narrow, dark hall with closed doors and a stair rising up. It was darker here than the shop and there was a strong smell of polish.

Polished linoleum, a shining, glass sea, with rugs scattered like islands. Not a speck of dust anywhere. Miss Evans looked down at their feet. "Better change into your slippers before we go up to your bedroom."

"We haven't got any," Carrie said. She meant to explain that there hadn't been room in their cases but before she could speak Miss Evans turned bright red and said quickly, "Oh, I'm so sorry, how silly of me, why should you? Never mind, as long as you're careful and tread on the drugget."

A strip of white cloth covered the middle of the stair carpet. They trod on this as they climbed; looking back from the top, Carrie saw the marks of their rubber-soled shoes and felt guilty, though it wasn't her fault. Nick whispered, "She thinks we're poor children, too poor to have slippers," and giggled.

Nina Bawden

TEXT

1 Why does Miss Evans not want a boy and a girl? Why do you think she changed her mind?

2 What sort of shop does Mr Evans own? Name three things that Carrie notices it sells.

3 Why do the children not have their slippers? Why does Miss Evans think they do not have slippers?

4 Say why you think there was white cloth on the stair carpet. How did Carrie feel when she had walked up the stairs? Give reasons.

5 Describe what you learn about Miss Evans from the passage, e.g. what she looks like, how she moves, how she behaves, what she says, what she thinks.

Say what impression this information gives you of the person.

6 Follow the same pattern and say what you learn about the character of Carrie.

SENTENCE

1 Use commas to separate the ideas in these sentences:

a) Having saved enough money we have decided to go on holiday now.

b) Enfield a suburb of London is where they have their shop.

c) Then standing to attention he took the salute.

d) The writer a man called Jones did not like the changes.

e) Jason the elder of the two brothers was blond.

f) Here in the ring two boxers each weighing sixteen stone snarled at each other.

g) The first pair who skated well were given full marks.

h) The streets already full were impossible to move through.

2 Write five more sentences of your own. Show how commas can be used to separate ideas. Use the sentences above to help you.

WORD

1 Put 'dis' before these verbs to make them negative. Check the spelling in a dictionary: appear, approve, appoint.

2 Write a sentence for each negative word in question 1 to show you understand what it means.

3 Put 'in' before these words to make them negative.
Check the spelling in a dictionary: audible, accurate, human.

4 Write a sentence for each negative word in question 3 to show you understand what it means.

5 Write a rule to say if the spelling changes when you make a word negative by adding a prefix.

Reynard the Fox

This poem takes the point of view of a fox,
Reynard, while he is being hunted. An 'earth' is
where a fox lives underground.

And here, as he ran to the huntsman's yelling,
The fox first felt that the pace was telling;
His body and lungs seemed all grown old,
His legs less certain, his heart less bold,
The hound-noise nearer, the hill-slope steeper
The thud in the blood of his body deeper.
His pride in his speed, his joy in the race,
Were withered away, for what use was pace?
He had run his best, and the hounds ran better,
Then the going worsened, the earth was wetter.
Then his brush drooped down till it sometimes dragged,
And his fur felt sick and his chest was tagged
With taggles of mud, and his pads seemed lead,
It was well for him he'd an earth ahead.
Within, as he reached that soft green turf,
The wind, blowing lonely, moaned like surf,
Desolate ramparts rose up steep
On either side, for the ghosts to keep.
He raced the trench, past the rabbit warren,
Close-grown with moss which the wind made barren;
He passed the spring where the rushes spread,
And there in the stones was his earth ahead.
One last short burst upon failing feet –
There lay life waiting, so sweet, so sweet,
Rest in a darkness, balm for aches.
The earth was stopped. It was barred with stakes.

John Masefield

TEXT

1 Give two facts from the poem to show that the fox is very tired.

2 What reason does the poet give about why the 'going worsened'? Even though it was more difficult, what kept the fox going?

3 What do you notice about the way this poem rhymes? Say where the rhymes come and what pattern they make.

4 The poem describes the fox running away from the dogs. When you read the poem, how does the rhythm and the rhyme help give you this picture? Give your reasons.

5 Write out the line, 'The thud in the blood ...'. Underline the onomatopoeic word and say what noise it makes.

6 How do you feel about the fox when you read the last line of the extract? Give your reasons for this. Who do you support in the poem – the fox or the hunters?

SENTENCE

1 Turn these phrases around and put in an apostrophe to show possession, e.g. the tail belonging to the fox – the fox's tail.

a) the hat belonging to Tracy
b) the hump belonging to the camel
c) the bottles belonging to the baby
d) the flames belonging to the fire

2 Put the apostrophe in the correct places in the following:

**my fathers overcoat   Dickens novels
two womens shopping
Marys skipping rope   two dogs tails**

3 Match words from column A and column B to make six pairs. Write them out using the apostrophe to show possession, e.g. the king's crown.

Column A	Column B
king	shell
cats	wheels
snail	whiskers
bicycle	hands
door	crown
clock	handles

WORD

1 Write these adjectives in three columns to show the comparison of adjectives.

e.g. cheap   cheaper   cheapest

strong big thin dry sad easy straight large grand brown

Check your spelling in a dictionary.

2 Say what the usual way of forming a comparative is, from your examples.

3 Copy and complete the chart with these adjectives: little, far, bad, many. Check your spelling carefully.

good	better	best

The People's Dispensary for Sick Animals

This is a part of an advertising leaflet for The People's Dispensary for Sick Animals (PDSA), a charity devoted to the care of animals and pets in distress.

OF THE HUNDREDS OF REASONS FOR SUPPORTING THE PDSA, HERE ARE JUST A FEW...

Every year over 1,400,000 treatments for animals in urgent need of veterinary care.

The charity was founded in 1917 and we now run a nationwide family of 45 community PDSA Centres.

To help further the work of the PDSA, we need to raise around £21.5 million every year.

The PDSA serves around 26,000 patients a year through private veterinary practices.

The PDSA is a registered charity and is completely self-financing. We receive no state aid and no lottery money. We depend entirely on gifts and donations.

On average it costs over £50 to cure a sick or injured pet.

In a typical day, the PDSA carries out 4,900 treatments at an average cost of more than £12.

It costs between £250,000 and £500,000 to build and equip each new PDSA Centre.

All of our resources are dedicated to treating animals in need. We do not accept healthy animals for neutering or cosmetic work.

TEXT

1 How many treatments were carried out at PDSA Centres last year? How much did this cost?

2 When was the charity founded? How many PDSA Centres are now working?

3 How do the PDSA receive most of the money that they need?

4 Who makes most use of PDSA services? What kinds of problems do they have to deal with?

5 What is the only way that the PDSA services can continue?

6 This advertising leaflet wants to persuade you to make a donation to the PDSA. Copy these ways in which they manage to do this:

Gives lots of statistics to show you the problem

Makes you feel sorry for animals

Makes you feel guilty for not paying

Find some examples in the passage. Add some more ways to the list.

SENTENCE

1 Use a dictionary and write the meanings of:
moreover, nevertheless, whereas.

2 Use them to join up these arguments:

a) I do not like people smoking. I would not ban smoking in public.

b) Some people think sunbathing is dangerous. My mum sits in the sun whenever possible.

c) Hunting whales is wrong. All whaling should be made illegal.

3 Use 'moreover', 'nevertheless' and 'whereas' in three argument sentences of your own.

4 Think of a subject you feel strongly about, e.g. wearing school uniform, pocket money, pollution. Write sentences arguing your point of view using these words:

**firstly   if   then   thus
therefore   so   whether
but   only if   however**

WORD

1 The PDSA appeals to your humanity. 'Humanity' is a noun formed from the adjective 'human'. Check in a dictionary and make nouns from these words:
sincere various active popular lovely generous

2 Make these words into nouns by adding a suffix from the box:
excite govern member king thorough amuse friend hero hard

ship   ment   dom   ness   ism

Check your spelling in a dictionary.

3 Write sentences using each of these words to show you understand their meanings.

Fog Poems

Both of these poems describe the fog in the form of a person. When this happens in writing, it is called 'personification'.

1. Slowly the fog

Slowly the fog,
Hunch-shouldered with a gray face,
Arms wide, advances,
Finger tips touching the way
Past the dark houses
And dark gardens of roses.
Up the short street from the harbour,
Slowly the fog,
Seeking, seeking;
Arms wide, shoulders hunched,
Searching, searching.
Out through the streets to the fields,
Slowly the fog –
A blind man hunting the moon.

F. R. McCreary

2. Mist

Subtle as an illusionist
The deft hands of the morning mist
Plays tricks upon my sight:
Haystacks dissolve and hedges lift
Out of the unseen fields and drift
Between the veils of white.
On the horizon, heads of trees
Swim with the mist about their knees,
And when the farm-dogs bark,
I turn to watch how on the calm
Of that white sea, the red-roofed farm
Floats like a Noah's Ark.

Douglas Gibson

TEXT

1 Write down one phrase from the start of each poem that describes the fog in human terms.

2 Describe how the fog moves in poem 1. Write down three or four words to describe this.

3 Explain why the fog is like an illusionist in poem 2. Give your reasons. Write down what you think are the characteristics an illusionist might have in common with fog.

4 Why does the poet describe the fog as 'a blind man hunting' in poem 1? Give your reasons.

5 Explain why the trees 'swim' and why the farmhouse should be 'like a Noah's Ark' in poem 2.

6 Read the poems again. *a)* Do you read them slowly or fast? *b)* Why are there so many 's' – sounding words in both poems? *c)* How do both of these features help you to get an impression of the fog?

SENTENCE

1 Join up these pairs of simple sentences using conjunctions such as 'when', 'before', 'as', 'although', 'so'.
a) Fred paused. He spoke. *b)* They heard a helicopter. They started to wave.
c) The sun came up. It became lighter. *d)* The room was freezing. We lit a fire.
e) The wheel had come off. That was a small problem.

2 Join a sentence from column A and a reason from column B using 'because'.

Column A	Column B
The bridge collapsed	The warm sun started to shine
My baby brother cried non-stop	It was not built well enough
I opened the windows wide	He was hungry for milk
Ray missed the bus	He got up late

3 Make up some sentences which join up two ideas using 'until', 'though', 'if', 'unless', 'before', e.g. I am not moving from this seat until I am sure we can return to it.

WORD

1 Write these words from the poems in alphabetical order.

a) finger, moon, blind, street, harbour, roses
b) tricks, sight, mist, trees, haystacks, veils, dogs, sea, farm, knees

2 Write the words in this list in alphabetical order:

whisper, whole, who, where, which, whether, whose

3 Here is a list of authors in this unit. Write them in alphabetical order by surname.
Anita Desai, Laura Ingalls Wilder, David McCord, J. W. Hackett, Ulli Beier, Nina Bawden.

Writing book reviews

Here are some ways of making book reviews more exciting.

1 Write a letter to the author of a book you have just read. Explain what you liked about the book or what you did not like. Say how you think it could have been better.

2 Put together a 'This Is Your Life' programme about one of the characters in the book.

3 Make a poster to advertise the book for the library.

4 Write the 'blurb' for the book – the words that are printed on the back cover. This should be short, but should make people want to read the book.

Changing your point of view

It is often interesting to use the same facts or details but to look at them from another person's point of view.

5 Read Unit 3.7 again. Imagine that you were someone on the station. Describe Miss Evans and what happens to Carrie and her brother.

◆ Fill in the background about Miss Evans – who she is, where she lives.

◆ Describe how you think she looks.

◆ Give some information about why Carrie and her brother are there.

◆ Say what you think Miss Evans' brother will say when he gets home.

6 Now write a description of Miss Evans as if you did not like her.

7 Read the poems in Unit 3.6 again. These are written from the point of view of the hunters. Imagine you are one of the animals. Write about what you think of the human beings and why. You could write it as a poem or a story.

8 The story of Reynard the Fox is told from the point of view of the fox. Write the same story as if you were the hunter.

◆ Describe the fox in front of you.

◆ What is the weather like? What is the countryside like?

◆ How do you feel about hunting and killing the fox?

◆ How do you feel when you know the fox is tired?

Describing characters

The way that characters are described makes us like or dislike them.

9 Imagine there was a robbery in the school. You saw the thief running away. Make a WANTED poster. Use adjectives from the Word box to describe the criminal. Look up the words in a dictionary. Find other words in a thesaurus.

> ### Word box
>
> *slovenly   plump   puny*
> *elegant   smart   stout*
> *unkempt   slim   huge*
> *shrivelled   lanky   moody*
> *spotty   wrinkled*

Do it like this:

WANTED

....

Age: about 35

Height: tall

Build: large and stocky

Any beard or moustache: black, shaggy beard

Shape of face: round and fat

Colour of hair: black

Shape of nose: pointy

Any distinguishing marks: scar on face

---

10 Choose a character from one of the sections in Unit 3. Imagine the character is missing or involved in a crime. Make a WANTED poster for him or her.

11 Now write about the character in a story of your own, but use adjectives which make him or her seem more attractive and friendly. Use a thesaurus.

Planning a book review

You must:

Explain to others what the book is about.

Make them so interested that they want to read it themselves.

Title and author

Give information so others can find the book.

Setting

Where do the story or events take place?

Plot

What happens in the story?

Do not give away what happens in the end!

Characters

Who are the people in the story?

What are they like?

How do you feel about them?

Do your feelings change? Why?

Finally

Say why you enjoyed the book.

Always give your reasons.

How are you getting on with things in the chart? If you need extra practice try the activities shown.

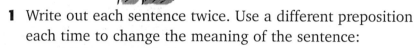

Grammar and punctuation	Prepositions	1
	Connecting words used in argument	2
	Combining sentences using connectives	3
	Commas to separate phrases and clauses	4
	Apostrophes – possession	5
Spelling, phonics and vocabulary	Words from other cultures	6
	Transforming words – negatives	7
	Transforming words – changing parts of speech	9

1 Write out each sentence twice. Use a different preposition each time to change the meaning of the sentence:

a) The railway line passes … the road.

b) Yesterday, I drove my car … the village.

c) The plane flew … Washington.

2 Use words such as 'thus', 'whereas' and 'whether' to join up these arguments:

a) Many people like zoos. I believe they should be closed.

b) People die from smoking every year. Cigarettes should be banned.

c) I can prove homework helps learning. Some people do not believe this.

3 Join the short sentences using connectives such as 'which', 'who', 'but' and 'and'.

a) I like my dog. I like my rat better.

b) My neighbour counts his money every night. He is very mean. He is very rich.

c) Amsterdam is a big city. It is in Holland. It has many canals.

4 Write out these sentences putting in the commas to separate the ideas:

a) Guy Fawkes the man who tried to blow up Parliament is the subject of my project.

b) Venice a city in Italy is famous for its canals.

c) Football a popular sport is played in all schools.

5 **a)** Turn these phrases around and put in an apostrophe to show possession, e.g.

the peak of the mountain – the mountain's peak:

the handle of the door   the kennel of the dogs   an ear of an elephant

b) Put the apostrophe in the correct places in the following:
two horses tails   St James church
a birds nest   the coats buttons   a snails shell

6 **a)** Use your dictionary to find out which countries gave us these words: khaki   coffee   pizza   tiger   barbecue   trek   caravan   bazaar   cola

b) Find out what these words mean: century   centipede cent   centurion.

What Latin word do they all have in common? What does it mean?

7 **a)** Put 'im' before these words to make them negative. Write a sentence for each to show you understand what they mean: polite   patient   perfect

b) Put 'un' before these words to make them negative. Write a sentence for each to show you understand what they mean: happy   qualified   equal

8 **a)** Make abstract nouns (qualities or feelings) from these adjectives:

e.g. adjective – beautiful: noun – beauty:

loyal   good   young   long   wide

b) Make verbs from these nouns or adjectives. Remember, you should be able to put 'to' in front of a verb,
e.g. noun – knee: verb – to kneel:

song   threat   bright   clean   action

9 Write the words in this list in alphabetical order:

vocation   virus   vogue   vertebra   vivacious   vengeance
brook   broke   broad   brown   brother   bromide

Handy hints for spelling

- Is the word spelt as it sounds? Does it contain any phonemes you already know?

- Does the word look right? Do you know any other words like it?

- Can you break the word into smaller parts? Which is the most difficult part of the word?

- Do you know what the word means?

- Have you used a word book or dictionary to help you?

LOOK SAY COVER WRITE CHECK

Glossary

adjective

An adjective is a describing word. It describes (adds meaning to) a noun.

the **big fat** cat

adverb

An adverb is a word or phrase which describes a verb.

He runs.   He runs **quickly**.

Many adverbs end in 'ly', but not all.

He runs **fast**.

agreement

Agreement is a link between two or more words in a sentence. It shows that they go together.

He shaved himself.

He and **himself** agree because they refer to the man.

Nouns in sentences should agree with the verbs. If you talk about one person or thing, your verb should be in the singular.

The **cat sits** on my knee.

If you talk about more than one thing, your verb should be in the plural form.

The **cats sit** on my knee.

antonym

An antonym is a word meaning the opposite, e.g. the antonym for **hot** is **cold**.

ambiguous

Words are ambiguous when they can have more than one meaning, for example, mummy can mean mother but when you study ancient Egypt it can mean something else!

Often ambiguous phrases are funny, like this newspaper headline:

BOY HITS GIRL WITH ICE CREAM

Is the girl hit with an ice cream by the boy or is the girl just carrying an ice cream when she is hit?

apostrophes for possession

If something belongs to someone, you show possession by using an apostrophe.

the cat's tail

The apostrophe shows that the tail belongs to the cat.

the dogs' bones

The apostrophe shows the bones belong to the dogs (plural).

Notice that apostrophes do not always come before the 's'. You should turn the sentence around using the word 'of', e.g. the tail of the cat, the bones of the dogs, to find where the apostrophe should come.

clause

A clause is a group of words. It can be used as a whole sentence or a part of a sentence. It must contain a verb.

It must have a subject. **Tracey** walked home.

it must have a verb.

cliché

A cliché is an expression which is used over and over again. It is often used in news reporting, and is not usually a very good description, e.g. 'sick as a parrot', 'as white as snow'.

conjunction

Conjunctions are joining words in sentences. They link ideas in a sentence.

She decided to go for a swim **because** she saw it was hot.

The commonest conjunctions are **and** and **but**.

connective

Connectives are words and expressions which can also join together ideas. Conjunctions can connect two ideas, but so can expressions such as 'in other words', 'finally', 'nevertheless', 'just then', 'as soon as possible'.

couplet

A couplet poetry, is where two lines following each other in a poem have the same kind of length and use the same rhyme. Couplet means a couple of lines.

The Mayor was dumb, and the Council stood
As if they had changed into blocks of wood.

dialogue

A dialogue is a conversation between two people. It can be spoken or written. If it is written, it will be set out like a playscript or must use the correct punctuation of speech.

direct speech

Direct speech refers to the words actually spoken in a conversation. When you write them down you need to use speech marks and set the speech out with a new speaker on each line.

'I like sweets,' he said.
'Well, I'm not buying you any,' replied mum.

figurative language

This is language which uses similes and metaphors (figures of speech) to create an impression or a mood.

She **flew** down the stairs.

The opposite of figurative language is when a description is literal – it describes something as it actually is.

He **flew** to Spain on a jet.

homograph

Homographs are spelt the same way but pronounced differently and mean completely different things.

My **bow** shoots arrows.
I **bow** to the Queen when I see her.

The **wind** was so strong it blew down the tree.
I can **wind** in the string of the kite.

homophone

Homophones are words that sound the same but are spelt differently. They also mean very different things:

paw, poor, pour

road, rowed, rode

idiom

An idiom is an expression used by people which is not literal (true). Idioms are used to make descriptions more interesting.

It rained cats and dogs.

imperative

An imperative verb is a command.

Get me a drink.

Switch on the TV.

We really mean: "**You** get me a drink", but we do not say the pronoun you.

instructional text

Instructional text is a piece of writing which aims to help you to do something successfully. It mostly gives you instructions.

metaphor

A metaphor is really a comparison of two things. The writer does not say one thing is *like* something else, but says it *is* something else.

He **is** an ass.

The moon is a ghostly galleon.

noun

A noun is a naming word. It can be the name of a person, place or thing (a common noun).
a girl   the park   a dragon.

It can be a proper noun – the name of a person, a particular place or thing. Proper nouns have capital letters.

France   Jenny

It can be a collective noun – the name of a group of things or people.

a swarm of bees   an army   a flock   a herd

Nouns can also be abstract – these are feelings or ideas.

love   jealousy   anger

onomatopoeia

Onomatopoeia words actually make the noise they are describing.

crackle

crash

pop

person of a verb

When writing, we can use verbs in:

Singular:

the **first person** – I said ... I make

the **second person** – you said ... you make

the **third person** – he said ... she said ... it makes

Plural:

the **first person** – We said ... we make

the **second person** – you said ... you make

the **third person** – they said ... they make

personification

Personification happens when a writer describes something as having the character or features of a human being.

The sun smiled on us today.

The fog crept through the streets.

phoneme

A phoneme is the smallest unit of sound in a word. It is not always a letter.

'Shoe' has two phonemes – 'sh' and 'oe'.

'Through' has two phonemes – 'thr' and 'ough'.

'Cat' has three phonemes – 'c' 'a' 't'.

phrase

A phrase is a part of a sentence. It usually consists of two or more words. It cannot make sense by itself as it does not have a verb.

against the wall

playscript

A playscript is a way of writing down dialogue for performance. The words for the actors are written down in a special way with stage directions. It is a different way from writing dialogue in a story. (See the unit on *Peter Pan*).

polysyllabic word

A polysyllabic word is a word with more than one syllable. 'Poly' comes from the ancient Greek word meaning 'many'.

prefix

A prefix is a group of letters we add to the beginning of a word to change its meaning. Happy – **un**happy

preposition

A preposition is a word which usually shows the position of one noun to another.

The cat sat **on** the mat.

The car drove **over** the bridge.

reported speech

Reported speech is the opposite of direct speech. In reported speech the writer is telling someone else what was said. Reported speech is sometimes called 'indirect speech'.

Direct speech: 'I like sweets,' she said.

Reported speech: She said that she liked sweets.

root of a word

The root is a word to which prefixes and suffixes can be added.

clear – **un**clear – clear**ly**

rhyme

A rhyme occurs when two words have an ending that sounds the same.

cat – hat   plane – rain.

simile

A simile is a comparison of two things. The writer says one thing is *like* another.

The sea is **like** a mirror.

suffix

A suffix is a group of letters added to the end of a word.

cook   cook**ing**   jump   jump**ed**

syllable

Smaller parts of longer words are called syllables.

<u>bad</u> has one syllable

<u>bad</u> – <u>min</u> – <u>ton</u> has three syllables.

synonym

Synonyms are words with the same meaning, or very similar meanings.

hot   boiling   steaming   scorching

tense of a verb

The tense of a verb tells us when something is happening: in the past, the present or the future.

Present: Now I **see** my mum

Past: Yesterday I **saw** my mum.

Future: Tomorrow I will **see** my mum.

thesaurus

A thesaurus is a book containing lists of synonyms. The words are arranged in alphabetical order.

verb

A verb is a doing or a being word.

The cat **scratched** my hand.

The cat **was** asleep.

High Frequency Word List

Term 1

baby
balloon
birthday
brother
children
clothes
garden
great
happy
head
heard
something
sure
swimming
those
word
work
world

Term 2

earth	own
eyes	paper
father	sister
friends	small
important	sound
lady	white
light	whole
money	why
mother	window

Term 3

Use this term to check up on spelling knowledge from previous terms.